Monmouth County
a Pictorial History

Robert F. Van Benthuysen
and Audrey Kent Wilson

Robt F. Van Benth (signature)

Audrey Kent Wilson (signature)

A limited edition of 3,000
of which this is number 2891.

D1244333

*First Jersey National Corporation
is proud to present this book
as our contribution to the
Monmouth County Tercentenary
We believe
that a thorough appreciation
of the past provides the best
insight into the future.
It is in this spirit
that we dedicate this history
to the accomplishments of yesterday,
the challenges of today
and the hopes of tomorrow.*

Thomas J. Stanton, Jr.
Chairman

Monmouth County
A Pictorial History

by Robert F. Van Benthuysen and Audrey Kent Wilson

Design by Jamie Backus Raynor
Donning Company/Publishers
Norfolk/Virginia Beach

This book is dedicated to the people of Monmouth County, past and present, who have labored unceasingly to make their county a pleasant place in which to live.

832760

Contents

Foreword

This year is a most appropriate date to publish a pictorial history of Monmouth County as 1983 marks the 300th anniversary of the founding of the county. On March 1, 1683, the first assembly under the proprietary government of East Jersey adopted laws setting up the courts and establishing the counties of Bergen, Essex, Middlesex, and Monmouth. The year 1983 will be marked by ceremonies and activities commemorating the event on the county and local level. In addition, the 1983-84 academic year will mark the fiftieth anniversary of the founding of Monmouth College, the first institution of higher education established in the county.

Audrey K. Wilson, the New Jersey librarian, and Robert F. Van Benthuysen, Director of the Guggenheim Memorial Library of Monmouth College, in this volume have assembled more than 300 pictures that tell the story of Monmouth County from the time when the Lenni Lenape Indians roamed the forests and coastal plain of Monmouth County to today when the county has become the home of many firms dealing in high technology.

The illustrations in this volume take the reader on a journey that covers 300 years of Monmouth County history. The reader will see and feel how the first settlers dealt with the native Americans, struggled to till the soil, and constructed the first rude structures that provided their housing. The photographs and the narrative emphasize the essential fact that the growth and development of this region resulted from the effort of hardworking people. The book captures the changes wrought by two world wars and the incidents, on a worldwide scale, that involved the lives of the youth of Monmouth County.

The photographs in *Monmouth County: A Pictorial History* show people at work and people at play; they show the places where people worshipped and worked. The volume shows in pictures the transition from an agricultural, rural countryside to the urban area, composed of fifty-three communities, that makes up Monmouth County today.

Despite all of the progress and the aspects of modern life revealed in the photographs, one can still discern the spirit of the first settlers, the courage of those who fought for our freedom at the Battle of Monmouth, and the vigor of the hardy fishermen who wrested a living from the sea.

This book gives us several hours hours of entertainment, pleasure, and a good bit of nostalgia. You may open the work at any page and find something of interest. It is the type of book that will be referred to again and again. To those who are Monmouth County natives this book will serve as a reminder of their past and to newcomers it will serve as an excellent introduction to the history of their adopted area. ●

Samuel Hays Magill, President
Monmouth College
West Long Branch, New Jersey

7

Preface

Those who love old photographs, with all their compelling magic, will find this pictorial history an enchanting collection. As though it was yesterday we see many of the scenes long vanished and the people now departed. The steamboat shown at the landing dock seems as though it will presently whistle, pull in its gangplank, and steam majestically away. A photograph is indeed the living past. Probably all the human faces are quite unknown, but there they are—smiling, frowning, pensive, or gay.

The chronological arrangement reconstructs the life of other eras. The photographs show how people dressed and wore their hair, what they did to enjoy themselves, and the jobs they performed; this is social history. The works represented tell us how things looked and how men lived in the past. The drawings give us personal interpretations of what the artists saw.

We have attempted to include as many unpublished and unfamiliar images as possible. However, certain photographs have become landmarks, and no compilation could afford to omit them. All the photographs were selected after extensive research. Many of them will evoke a dozen different images for as many individual viewers, or suggest others that might just as well have been included. Occasionally one may detect a flow of history from a single photograph.

For the most part the photographers are unknown, but one may easily discern the touch of the professional as well as the naivete of the earnest amateur. Many of the photographs appear to be the product of pure chance or of an individual bent on catching in permanent form evidence of his or her time. We are indebted to these photographers and illustrators who have enriched our lives.

"The mirror of memory" is what the enthusiastic amateur photographer Oliver Wendell Holmes called the camera. What we have attempted to present is a warm evocation of bygone memories, a family album showing Monmouth County's traditional life and the changes that have inexorably altered its character.

No work that has the scope of this volume could have been completed without the assistance of many persons vitally interested in Monmouth County history. We are grateful to Dr. Peter J. Guthorn, Samuel Stelle Smith, and George H. Moss, Junior, caretakers of Monmouth County history, whose enthusiasm and expertise have simplified our project.

Fellow librarians and associates— Olga Boeckel, of the Register Library; Gertrude Hooker, of the Red Bank Public Library; Dolores McKeough, of the Matawan-Aberdeen Public Library; Jean Cervellino, of the Freehold Borough Library;

Charles Cummings and Bob Blackwell, of the Newark Public Library; Jack Livingstone, of the Monmouth County Library; and J. Louise Jost, of the Shrewsbury Historical Society— have all opened their collections to us. We are indebted for their cooperation and goodwill.

We are thankful to Jane Grammer, photographer and former library associate, whose joy is documenting the social aspects of the county; Tom Hoffman, National Park Service Ranger at Gateway National Recreation Area, Sandy Hook, whose love of history is preserving and telling the story of that spit of land; and to Rita Nannini, professional photographer, who here portrays the lives of one ethnic group.

Special gratitude is expressed to those who worked unstintingly with us: to Jeff Lega and Charles H. Maps, Jr., whose devotion to the art and skill of photography have eased our way; and to Dolores Schibell, whose skilled fingers produced the manuscript copy.

As our deadline grew closer we realized that it was necessary to say, "we must stop here," even though there are many more items of historical interest we would like to include. As with any book of history, some will remark that a particular subject or person was omitted or incompletely covered. The authors accept full responsibility for any omissions. ●

This replica of the *Half Moon,* Henry Hudson's ship, was sent to the United States in honor of the 300th anniversary of Hudson's discovery of North America. In 1609 Hudson sailed from Amsterdam, and on September 1 Robert Juet recorded their landfall in Monmouth County. Courtesy of Samuel Stelle Smith

The Italian navigator Giovanni da Verrazano (1485-1525) was the son of Pier Andrea di Bernardo da Verrazano. Sailing for Francis I of France, Verrazano set out from Dieppe on the *Dauphine* in 1524. He is believed to have entered Sandy Hook Bay and come in contact with the Lenni Lenape Indians in the Highlands area. Verrazano served Francis I as a privateer, attacking Spanish shipping. It is believed that he was killed by the native of the West Indies crica 1527. Courtesy of Samuel Stelle Smith

The Ground We Stand On

"This is a very good Land to fall with and a pleasant Land to see."

These words documented in a journal kept by Robert Juet, a gentleman of dubious position aboard Henry Hudson's *Half Moon,* described Monmouth County in 1609. What Juet observed were the Highlands of the Neversink (Navesink). Behind these verdant promontories lay miles of flatlands, valleys, and rolling hills. Fish and shellfish teemed in the clear ocean waters which coursed into swiftly running rivers and sheltered bays. Tea-colored streams snaked through woods which were brimming with deer, turkey, and other small game. The forests of pines lying over pure, sweet water yielded nuts, roots, berries, and herbs.

Monmouth County is bordered on the east by the Atlantic Ocean, and the Sandy Hook and Raritan bays to the north; it abuts Middlesex and Mercer counties to the west, and Ocean County (until 1850 part of Monmouth County) to the south. The area is dotted with hills

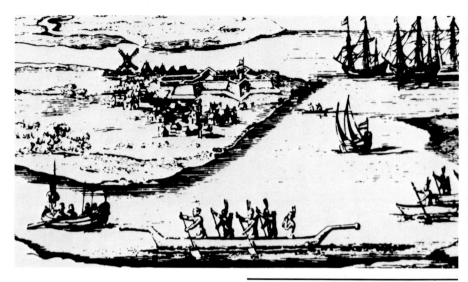

ranging in elevation from 30 to 400 feet above sea level. Two principal rivers, the Navesink (or North Shrewsbury) and the South Shrewsbury, rise from a network of brooks in the northwestern portion of the county, and broaden to become bays before merging to flow into Sandy Hook Bay. The rivers' courses are dotted with small, grassy islands, and the banks are sandy or lined with sedgy marshes.

A number of small western creeks and brooks channel into three rivers, the Shark, the Manasquan, and the Metedeconk, which empty into the ocean.

The Indian, caribou, woolly mammoth, and the mastodon were coexistent. The Paleo-Indian survived the cold climate of the last ice age and lived in migratory fashion following the game, his food. The skillfully made stone implements found lead to conjecture about the conditions under which he lived, hunted, sheltered, and clothed himself.

An artifact found at Turkey Swamp as a result of excavations by the Archaeological Society of New Jersey, Monmouth County Chapter, has pushed the date of Indian habitation back 10,000 years. This tool, a point with Paleo and Early Archaic attributes, places the Indian in Monmouth County around 9,000 B.C.

The site at Turkey Swamp, a sandy-soil, dense, piney forest area on the Manasquan River, was probably a temporary encampment used seasonally by the nomads for hunting and gathering food. Tools of later dates were recovered in the stratified soil, indicating that the camp was used repeatedly over the years. Charred animal bones and seeds were unearthed from a hearth. Artifacts characteristic of food processing and the production of clothing were excavated. Spears, points, flints, butcher tools, and anvil stones were found in the granular soil, which has been pene-

trated to a depth of fifty-five inches.

This location was the stopping place of the wandering Paleo, Archaic, and Woodland peoples from 10,000 B.C. to 1700 A.D. Many of the tools found were made of materials not indigenous to the area, signifying either a network of trading enterprises or a greater range of migratory travels, or both. The site also records the changing and perfecting technology the Indian used in the manufacture of his utensils and implements.

Turkey Swamp is not the only Indian site in Monmouth County, but the excavation is the most expertly organized and documented. Tools have been recovered from farmlands and other temporary campsites along the sandy margins of river and creek beds.

By the time the explorers Giovanni de Verrazzano and Henry Hudson observed their first native Americans, the climate had moderated; the land was more hospitable to the small family bands of Indians. They were the Lenni Lenape, part of the Algonquin nation and named "Delawares" by the early settlers because of their concentration on the Delaware River, New Jersey's western boundary. The Indians shared a common language and culture and lived in small autonomous groups in scattered settlements.

The American Indians, viewed as savages by the explorers and

As a result of Henry Hudson's voyage the Dutch traders arrived in New York. The United New Netherland Company was granted a three-year monopoly on trade in 1614. Then Dutch East India Company received a twenty-year exclusive trade agreement in 1621. This early picture portrays the fort settlement at New Amsterdam. From this point the Dutch traded with the Indians in New Jersey. Courtesy of Samuel Stelle Smith

colonists, were an intensely religious people. They worshipped a supreme deity and a multitude of lesser gods; these lesser gods were the keepers of the animals and the agents for the movement of the seasons. Their benevolence was demonstrated by adequate rainfall and abundant harvests.

With the stabilization of the climate, comparable to today's, larger groups lived in settlements, adding fishing and farming to their food gathering activities.

Indians from other parts of New Jersey and Pennsylvania followed the Minisink and Burlington paths, early trails which terminated at Monmouth's shoreline.

Hostile relations existed between the Indians and the Dutch, the first settlers; some blood was spilled. The second wave of colonizers, the English, pursued a policy of "buying" the land, a concept the Indians never understood, for the land was akin to the moon, stars, and the sea. If the Indians resisted, the settlers resorted to debilitating whiskey, blankets

Sir George Carteret was born on the island of Jersey in 1599. In 1664, with Lord Berkeley, he became a proprietor of East Jersey and gave the name of Nova Caesaria or New Jersey to his holdings in America. Courtesy of Samuel Stelle Smith

impregnated with smallpox, and finally, guns.

During a succession of colonial wars, France and England were fighting for supremacy in the old and new world. During the French and Indian conflict (1754-1763) the two European armies and the Indians favorable to either side were pitted against rival colonists.

In New Jersey, between 1756 and 1758, settlers were prey to French-inspired Indian attacks. Homes were destroyed, and hundreds of colonists were slain or scalped. New Jersey governor Jonathan Belcher appointed a commission to call a conference with Indian leaders to discuss land which the Indians claimed had never been purchased. Meanwhile, the general assembly passed a law requiring all able men from ages sixteen to sixty to arm themselves. A blockhouse was built at Middletown at the present site of Christ Episcopal Church, with a detail of six armed men quartered there to alert the inhabitants against surprise attacks.

The conferences at Crosswicks heard the disputes, treaties were signed, and the assembly set aside monies to settle land and fishing claims.

All the tools of intimidation were in the white men's hands; Indians began to migrate westward, some north to Canada. By 1758 there were only about 500 Indians living in New Jersey, and of these 60 to 100

This map dated between the years 1683 and 1685 illustrates the proximity of Gravesend, Long Island to Middletown and Shrewsbury and the relative ease with which the Patentees came in search of land. The settlements of Middletown, Portland, Sandy Pointe (Sandy Hook), and the ironworks at the Falls of the Shrewsbury are represented. Courtesy of Samuel Stelle Smith

13

were living on a reservation in South Jersey.

The Indians were peaceful, claimed Arnold Rock, who was one of the last Lenni Lenape Indians in Monmouth County. In the 1970s Rock stated that not one man was scalped in New Jersey and that the Indian had been a good friend to the settler, teaching him to grow corn, pumpkins, potatoes, and tobacco, and to survive the hard winters.

The oral tradition of a variously told legend contradicts Rock's statements. In 1620 Penelope Van Princis and her husband were bound for New Amsterdam on a ship loaded with Dutch settlers when the ship ran aground on Sandy Hook. Penelope's husband was weak from having been ill most of the voyage, and could not travel far by foot. Fearful of Indian attacks, the ship's passengers headed for Manhattan Island, leaving Penelope and her young husband on the beach alone.

Hostile Indians attacked, killing Penelope's husband, and left her wounded. (They thought she was dead.) She crawled into a hollow tree and survived by eating bark and frozen tree gum until two braves found her some time later. The older Indian saved Penelope from the young, brash brave who would have killed her.

The story continues that Mrs. Van Princis was taken to an Indian village not too far away. When word reached New Amsterdam of a white woman living among the Indians, the settlers concluded that she was the missing Penelope, and set out for what is present-day Middletown to ransom her with beads, scissors, cloth, and bracelets; their mission was a success. Mrs. Van Princis eventually returned to Monmouth County as the wife of Richard Stout, an Englishman. Many hundreds of their descendants still live in Monmouth County. ●

Richard Hartshorne, a Middletown settler, wished to use the land on Sandy Hook for grazing and leased it from Berkeley and Carteret, the proprietors of New Jersey. The Indians who hunted on the land, used the trees for canoes, and picked the berries, became troublesome. In 1677, under this tree in Middletown, Hartshorne made an agreement with Indian leader, Vowavapon, to buy Sandy Hook for thirteen shillings. Courtesy of Samuel Stelle Smith

14

This is a lithographic copy of a painting by Granville Penn, a descendant of William Penn. He painted this portrait of Lenni Lenape chief Lap-pa-win-so in 1737. This painting is one of two portraits of Delaware Indians rendered by the artist. The pouch around the Indian chief's neck holds his ceremonial pipe. Courtesy of Samuel Stelle Smith

The Old Yellow Meeting House on Red Valley Road in Upper Freehold Township was erected in 1737. An offshoot of the Baptist Church in Middletown, it is of frame construction with clapboard siding, a rectangular, gabled roof, interior chimneys, and shuttered window openings. The church exemplifies early religious life in rural Monmouth County. Photo courtesy the Monmouth County Historical Association

The *Monmouth County Family Tree* was created by Samuel Stelle Smith, historian and author from Monmouth Beach. The tree illustrates the formation of the fifty-three municipalities of the county. Smith's books dealing with Monmouth County's history are *Sandy Hook and the Land of the Navesink* and *The Battle of Monmouth*. He has also done extensive research on Molly Pitcher, the heroine of the Battle of Monmouth. Courtesy of Samuel Stelle Smith

15

The King's Highway was widened by edict in 1719, to be used as a military or post road. From surveys made in 1769 in Middletown, the road was six rods wide, without tolls or barriers. Riding

chapter 2

No Time For Rest: 1663-1774

Henry Hudson, an Englishman, was sponsored by the Dutch, and his voyage of discovery gave the Dutch title to land in New Jersey. Being traders and trappers, they were slow to establish settlements in Monmouth County. In 1690 Dutch settlers began to arrive from Long Island. In 1663 a group of Englishmen from Long Island sailed their sloop across the bay to Monmouth County to purchase lands for settlement. After repeated visits the landseekers settled on three "necks" of land which included the area between Raritan Bay and the town of Port-au-peck on the south branch of the Shrewsbury River. The Indians called these lands Newasink, Navarumsunk, and Pootapeck. Newasink extended from the bay and the Navesink Highlands, which included the areas that became the towns of Navesink, Middletown, and Highlands. A tract of land at Sandy Hook was reserved for Indian food collection activities. The Navarumsunk portion included the land between the Navesink and Shrewsbury

Rivers which included one of the original Monmouth County settlements, Shrewsbury. The Pootapeck lands were south of the South Shrewsbury River. These lands had been purchased from the Indians with guns, clothing, tobacco, wine, and peague (money made from shells). By the spring of 1664 John Bowne, Richard Stout, and three other families were living in Middletown.

In 1664 Peter Stuyvesant surrendered New Amsterdam to the English, and a year later, by the authority of the Duke of York, Governor Nicholls issued a proclamation to initiate new settlements. The conveyance, called the Monmouth Patent, included all of present-day Monmouth County, and parts of Middlesex and Ocean counties.

The terms set forth by the document assured the colonizers that the land, which was to be planted and cultivated within three years, was free land. It was exempt from taxation for the first five years, and then only to be taxed for public purposes, to provide for their minister, and civil and military officials. All the land was to be purchased from the Indian sachems and registered with the governor. The guarantee of religious freedom attracted many settlers from Massachusetts and Rhode Island who had been persecuted for their beliefs.

In 1670 at a meeting of the Monmouth patentees full rights and claims under the patent were offered to the county's first settlers; their names were added to the list of associates.

As a result of the colonization effort, in 1670 there were more than the required 100 families required by the patent. The beginnings were arduous: homes were built of crude logs, with oiled paper for windows; the work in the fields was hard and repetitious. The settlers were plagued by disease, mosquitoes, and fleas, and the boring sameness of the food.

By 1700 Middletown was bustling with mills, stores, and a blacksmith shop. Houses were built for show and comfort. Meal, flour, beef, and pork were available from the markets of the growing city of New York. A children's school had been established, perhaps the first in the colony. Indian paths were widened to permit horses, and the colonists were able to travel, visit, and to choose acreage outside the villages for farming. Taverns or "ordinaries" began to spring up for the comfort of the traveler.

South of Middletown, along the King's Highway at the intersection of the Burlington Path, lay the village of Shrewsbury. One of its earliest settlers, James Grover, built his ironworks at the "Falls of Shrewsbury." Some time between 1665 and 1676 Grover sold the works to the man who had suggested the name of the county, Colonel Lewis Morris from Monmouthshire, England. Morris, a former commander under Cromwell, named his estate Tintern Manor. (Today it is called Tinton Falls.) In twenty years the few original settlers grew to over 100 and transformed the wilderness into cultivated land of over 1,000 acres.

The county's first settlers adopted the town meeting as their form of government. The business of local government was limited to the building of roads, property demar-

Richard Hartshorne was a Quaker who came to Middletown in 1667. The original portion of his home was built prior to 1685, and consisted of one low-ceilinged room with a large brick walk-in fireplace. The surrounding plantation of 2,000 acres belonged to Hartshorne, whose brother William was one of the proprietors of East Jersey and a patentee of Monmouth County. The land was purchased from the Indians, and the Battle of Navesink, a skirmish during the Revolution, was fought within sight of the house. Courtesy of the Monmouth College Library

18

Not all settlers could live in this elegant or gracious style, nor did the Taylor family in the seventeenth century. This addition to the homestead, now called Marlpit Hall, was built in the 1700s. The thirteen-room house, owned by the Monmouth County Historical Association, is located on King's Highway in Middletown. Seven of the rooms in this seventeenth to eighteenth century house are open to the public. Courtesy of the Monmouth College Library

cation, and local laws. Members of the town meeting selected representatives to the general assembly, whose concern was the whole province. By 1693 the population had increased enough to divide the county into three townships, and the assembly created Freehold on the western route of the Burlington Path, the Indian trail.

In 1685 a group of exiled Scotch Presbyterians who called themselves Covenanters, or Dissenters, found the land around Freehold fertile, the rainfall abundant, and excellent stands of timber for homebuilding. They called their land New Aberdeen.

The first courts were held in 1667 at Middletown. By 1670 the courts alternated between Shrewsbury and Middletown and met two days each year. Later, in 1713, Freehold (then called Monmouth Court House) was selected as the central seat of government. The new courthouse was built in 1715 on Main Street, the Burlington Path in Freehold.

Demonstrating loyalty was difficult for the settlers because the ownership and government of New Jersey changed hands often. In 1670 the Duke of York gave his friends, John Lord Berkeley and Sir George Carteret, the proprietorship of New Jersey, and in 1672 some delegates from the town meetings established a new government under Captain George Carteret, the son of Sir

George. The Dutch regained control for a few months in 1673 and once the colony returned to British ownership, it had two additional owners. First, John Fenwick in 1674; and then William Penn and his twelve associates in 1681.

Commencing with the Berkeley-Carteret rule, the new proprietors denied the validity of the Monmouth Patent and levied taxes and "quit rents." The patentees and other settlers claimed exemptions, resisting the proprietors' claims to ownership. Land riots and lawsuits resulted. In Freehold in 1769-1770 the farmers assembled in front of the courthouse and refused entry to the lawyers and magistrates. Money was in short supply and their farms were being foreclosed. This situation existed until the Revolutionary War, and many of the problems remained unresolved afterwards.

Monmouth County, bent upon its agricultural pursuits in 1774, was far removed from the sites of conflict, but the inhabitants were alarmed that the acts of suppression would soon be enforced countrywide. The Monmouth County colonists were sympathetic—it was time to choose sides. ●

In 1665, James Grover, a patentee, built a grist mill (shown here) at the Falls of Shrewsbury. The rights to the mineral springs at the site were reserved for the Indians. Two years later Grover and his associates began to score the bogs for valuable iron ore. This was the first iron mining enterprise in New Jersey. By 1680 the new owner, Colonel Lewis Morris, had an extensive ironworks in operation with around seventy black slaves who were housed on the estate.

The building, with solid oak columns and its beams resting in bedrock, was used as a flour mill in 1880. The dam was smashed by ice in 1927 and the mill closed. The building, home for the arts and theatre in the last few decades, is now a dinner theatre called the Dam Site. Courtesy of the Monmouth College Library

Old Mill, Eatontown, N. J.

Interior of Old Mill, Eatontown, N. J.

Eaton Mill was built by Thomas Eaton in 1670 as a grist mill. Eaton ran his mill until he died in 1688. His widow presumably carried on until 1710, when her only surviving son, John, inherited the business. The mill later became known as "Richmond's Mill." It survived long into the industrial age and was not demolished until the 1920s. A marker on Highway 35 in Eatontown shows the site of the mill. Courtesy of the Monmouth College Library

21

In response to the needs of travelers, taverns and inns sprang up along the paths and stage roads. One of the oldest, and still catering to the joy and comfort of the public, is the Our House Tavern on the Freehold Road in Ardena. The sign above the door dates the building to 1747.

Gossip, politics, and news were aired in the colonial taverns. They were usually the site of the early town meetings, and probably much treasonable language against the Crown. Today the Our House Tavern is one of Monmouth's fine restaurants; its three dining rooms seat seventy-five. The menu is limited, but excellent, and the specialty of the house is fowl. Courtesy of the Monmouth College Library

Hunns Tavern, or the Hawkins House, is traced by deed to 1761. John Reid made the original land survey in 1701, and the house stands on land owned by Thomas and Stephen Warne, the former a proprietor of East Jersey. The house passed through many owners, and records show that Mrs. Hunn ran a small shop. Her grandson Thomas was a major in the Revolutionary War. He was tried for cowardice and cashiered at a court-martial in Freehold in September 1780.

Purportedly used as a hospital after the Battle of Monmouth, the house passed to John Hunn, Thomas's brother who was a private in the Revolution. John's son, Peter, married Philip Freneau's sister, Margaret. Two

local legends are attached to the house. After his "vision" and consequent sickness, the Reverend William Tennent reverted to childhood and relearned to read and write here. Later the house was a stop on the underground railroad—a crawl space under the floor was used to hide escaped Negro slaves. Courtesy of the Monmouth College Library

This tavern was established in colonial days in response to legislation ordering the establishment of taverns or "ordinaries." Willow Tree Tavern became the home of Tobias Hendrickson and his wife Margaret Perrine. The village was called Perrineville for the family who settled the area to farm. The Perrines, Huguenots who came in 1665 to avoid persecution, were indentured to Carteret. Many of the Perrine men fought with the Continentals. Courtesy of the Monmouth College Library

22

The Hawkins House stood on lot number eight of the original twenty-four plotted out in 1701 by John Reid, surveyor-general and Quaker agent for the proprietors of East Jersey. Reid also made his home in the Mount Pleasant settlement. The plots were 40 feet, 9 inches wide and 4,800 feet long.

The Scots who settled here named their holdings New Aberdeen. The town name later was changed to Middletown Point, signifying its importance as the shipping terminus for the Middletown settlement. Mrs. Marian Hawkins, a descendant of the original settler, is seen with friends in this picture. Courtesy of the Aberdeen-Matawan Public Library

The Derrick Longstreet House was built by a retired sea captain in 1765. It is the oldest house in Brielle and one of two left standing when the Tories burned the saltworks at Brielle, then called Union Landing. Because of the 200-year-old boxwood trees which surround the place, it is now called Boxwood Cottage. The wooden dwelling has beamed ceilings and two large fireplaces. Many prominent people have lived here, among them the artist Ellen Churchman and Robert Louis Stevenson. Courtesy of the Monmouth College Library

Cemeteries may be important historical and social resources and their preservation has been carried out by many local volunteer groups. A good example of a preserved gravestone is that of Margaret Kerr who "departed this life" in 1731. Courtesy of the *Register*

23

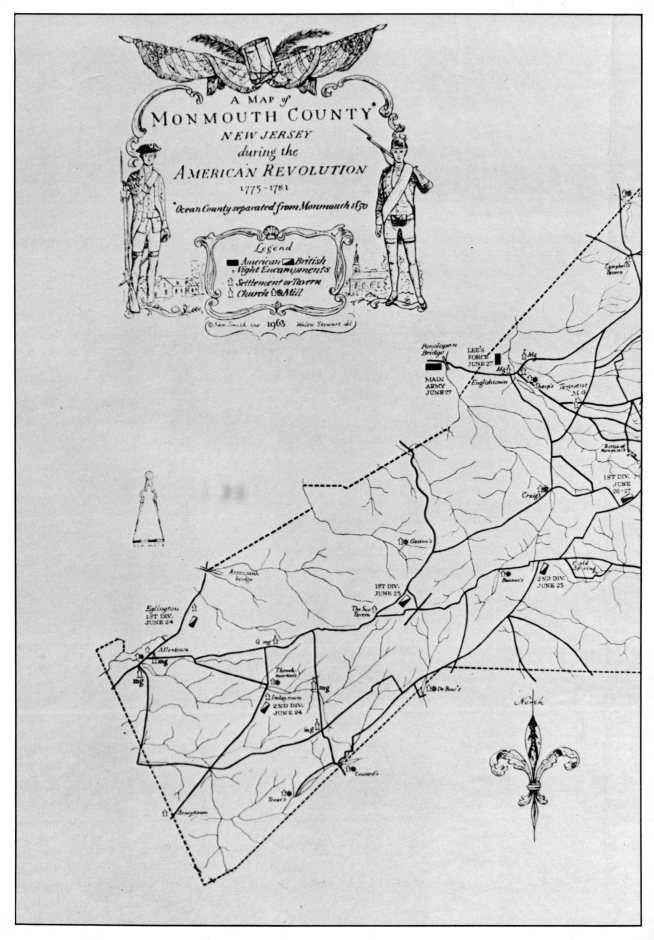

A MAP of MONMOUTH COUNTY NEW JERSEY during the AMERICAN REVOLUTION 1775-1781

Ocean County separated from Monmouth 1850

Legend
■ American ◣ British Night Encampments
⌂ Settlement or Tavern
⛪ Church ⚙ Mill

© Sam Smith inv 1963   Walter Stewart del

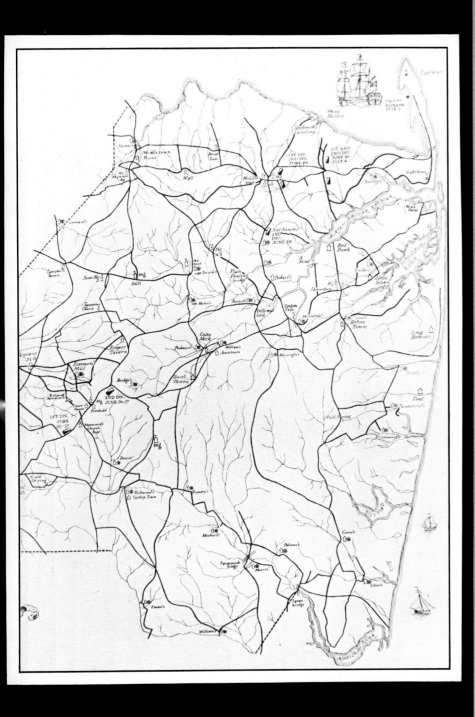

Shown here is a map of Monmouth County during the American Revolution. Map prepared by and photo courtesy of Samuel Stelle Smith

The Winning Of Freedom: 1775~1800

New Jersey claims the title "The Cockpit of the Revolution," and the center of the cockpit was Monmouth County. Its long coastline, stretching from Perth Amboy on Raritan Bay in the north, to Egg Harbor Inlet in the south, made it a particularly exposed position to defend. This fact, coupled with the number of Tories in the area, made it vulnerable to material devastation, military conflict, and civil war. In January 1775, the Tories of Shrewsbury refused to form a "committee of inspection" as directed by the provincial congress. They were then forced to do so by their neighbors at Freehold and elsewhere, but they gave only lip service.

By July 1776 Monmouth County teemed with plots to assist the British. Armed parties of "Pine Robbers," as the Patriots called them, lurked among the pines and dunes along the coast. The "Robbers" kept in touch with landing parties from British ships, helped their foraging parties, supplied them with information about Patriot numbers and movements, and made life dangerous for the Patriot detachments assigned to guard the coast and drive the cattle inland out of reach of foragers. The people of the coastal areas of the county lived in continual fear of British plunder and Loyalist retaliation. The Tories' hanging of Captain Joshua Huddy on the shore of the Highlands, on April 12, 1782, symbolized the violence and brutality in revolutionary Monmouth County.

The first battle between American and British troops in Monmouth County occurred on February 13, 1777, near the lighthouse on the Navesink Highlands—then called Neversink, or Nevesink. The engagement was disastrous for the First Regiment of the Monmouth Militia, commanded by Colonel Nathaniel Scudder. A British force of 170 men from Staten Island, commanded by Major Andrew Gordon, caught the untrained militia by surprise.

British accounts listed twenty-five militiamen killed, seventy-two captured, and an unknown number wounded. Many of those captured later died in the infamous Liberty Street Sugar House in New York, which was used as a British prison.

The war reached Monmouth with a vengeance on a hot June day in 1778. When the Crown learned that France had acknowledged the independence of the United States and had promised military help, the British decided to give up Philadelphia and unite its divided forces in New York. At Valley Forge, Washington learned of the British plan and began preparations to disrupt any attempt to consolidate the British Army. The two adversaries met at Monmouth Court House on June 28, 1778.

Washington gave General Charles Lee command of the American forces, but Lee's initial activities were dilatory, giving Sir Henry Clinton, the British commander, time to prepare for a general action.

Emerging from his winter encampment at Valley Forge, Washington crossed the Delaware near Lambertville and maneuvered to cut off the enemy's push through New Jersey. On June 28, 1778 he rallied General Lee's advance forces as they were retreating from Monmouth Court House. The Commander-in-Chief then forced Sir Henry Clinton to withdraw from the fields near Old Tennent Church. Searing heat during the longest engagement of the Revolutionary War added to the toll on both sides. Photo courtesy of the Monmouth College Library

26

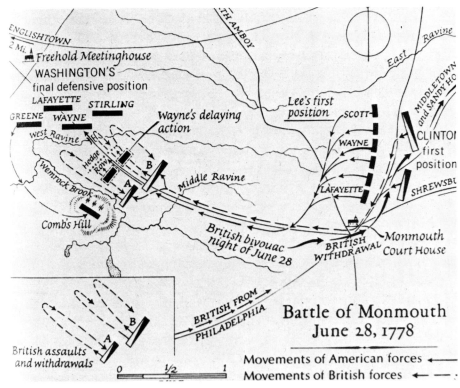

Battle of Monmouth
June 28, 1778

Movements of American forces ←———
Movements of British forces ←— —·

This map shows troop movements at the Battle of Monmouth, June 28, 1778. Photo courtesy of the Monmouth College Library

Washington then took command of the attacking force after sternly rebuking Lee. This was supposedly the one time in his life when the Father of Our Country was heard to swear in public. For the first time the Americans fought well with the bayonet as well as with the musket and rifle, and their battlefield behavior generally reflected the training received at Valley Forge.

During most of the afternoon, in temperatures reaching 100 degrees, British troops under Baron von Knyphausen and Lieutenant Colonel Henry Monckton repeatedly attacked the American forces, to no avail. After attempting an invasion of the center of the American line, Clinton ordered a withdrawal to a defensible position. Washington prepared to attack, but darkness ended the fighting. During the night Clinton's army retreated to Middletown, and later to Sandy Hook, where it boarded transport vessels for New York City. Both sides suffered heavy casualties, caused as much by the heat and fatigue as by the battle.

Among the prominent Americans in the battle that day were Generals Lord Stirling (William Alexander), Nathanael Greene, Anthony Wayne, Charles Scott, and their French ally, General Lafayette. Monmouth was the last general engagement in the north between the armies of Washington and Clinton.

The battle is probably best remembered for the gallant deeds performed by one of the most popular heroines of the Revolution, Molly Pitcher (really Mary Ludwig Hays). Molly carried water to the thirsty American cannoneers. She was on the field at the side of her husband, John Hays, who was a gunner in Captain Francis Proctor, Junior's company of artillery attached to the Pennsylvania line. When her husband John was wounded, Molly stepped up to replace him at the cannon.

Following the battle, Washington reported to Henry Laurens, president of the Continental Congress, "We forced the enemy from the field and encamped on their grounds." To his brother Augustine he wrote, "from an unfortunate and bad beginning [it] turned out a glorious and happy day."

On April 14, 1783 Congress proclaimed war's end, and Monmouth County residents welcomed the news with mingled solemnity and joy. Church bells rang out from Freehold to Middletown, and over the vast reaches of Shrewsbury Township; ministers called congregations together in thanksgiving. No doubt many glasses of "Jersey lightning" were lifted in heartfelt toasts to an independent nation.

The next item of business was to put in order wasted fields and torched homes, churches, and barns. Buildings could be rebuilt, but the gap that inevitably had opened between those who had become revolutionists and those who had remained loyal to Great Britain was difficult to bridge. Many Monmouth County people of Loyalist persuasion had fled to New York City, and at war's end they wanted to return, forgiven, to resettle their lands. But many who dared to return were insulted, abused, and coated with tar and feathers. ●

27

As senior officer in Washington's army, General Charles Lee was placed in command of an advance force of 5,000 men at the Battle of Monmouth. Lee's failure to develop a plan of attack during the initial stages of the battle resulted in a retreat by the American force. He was later court-martialed for his actions that day. Photo courtesy of the Monmouth College Library

The Marquis de Lafayette, our French ally and a major general in Washington's army, was only twenty-one years of age when he participated in the Battle of Monmouth; he commanded three regiments and defended Washington's left flank. Photo courtesy of the Monmouth College Library

Brigadier General Henry Knox was in over-all charge of the American artillery at the Battle of Monmouth. Following the battle he expressed delight with the coolness, bravery, and good conduct of his men, and he wrote that evening to his wife "that no artillery could have been better served that ours." Courtesy of the Monmouth College Library

Aaron Burr, the third vice president of the United States, commanded a brigade during the Monmouth campaign. Following the battle he openly sided with Charles Lee in the controversy that followed. This portrait was painted by Gilbert Stuart. Photo courtesy of the New Jersey Historical Society

Alexander Hamilton, Washington's trusted advisor, served as the General's aide-de-camp at the Battle of Monmouth. In 1804 Hamilton was killed in a duel with Aaron Burr, who also had fought in the battle. This portrait was painted by Charles Wilson Peale. Hamilton wears across his chest the green sash that identifies an aide-de-camp, and on his shoulder the epaulettes of a lieutenant colonel. Photo courtesy of the Frick Art Reference Library

28

This famous painting by Emanuel Leutze (1816-1868) was painted in 1857. It hangs in the Monmouth County Historical Association Museum in Freehold. The painting depicts General George Washington at the moment he intercepted General Charles Lee about a mile east of Tennent Meetinghouse early in the afternoon of Sunday, June 28, 1778. General Lee had spent several hours up front with approximately 5,000 Continental troops and militia. First he had advanced against the British rear guard, then retreated in a manner which Washington considered "a breach of orders." On horseback, behind General Washington, are Major General Marquis de Lafayette and Lieutenant Colonel Alexander Hamilton. Photo courtesy of Samuel Stelle Smith

This oil painting is signed Dennis Carter, 1856. It portrays Molly Pitcher being presented to General Washington on the field at the Battle of Monmouth. No documented information regarding this meeting has been found, but this is not proof that it did not happen. Photo courtesy of the Monmouth County Historical Association

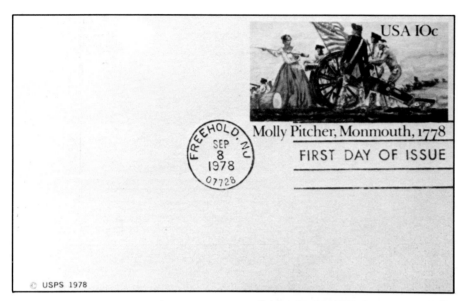

© USPS 1978

The United States Postal Service issued a special commemorative postal card in 1978 to honor Molly Pitcher and to mark the 200th anniversary of the Battle of Monmouth. Photo courtesy of the Monmouth College Library

According to some historians the Englishtown Inn on the corner of Water and North Main streets in Englishtown served as Washington's headquarters during the Battle of Monmouth. The court-martial orders of General Charles Lee were prepared here following the battle. The building is a framed, shingled, two-story structure with gabled roof, interior end chimneys, and a full-width porch. It is currently undergoing restoration. Photo courtesy of Samuel Stelle Smith

The Covenhoven House on West Main Street in Freehold served as British General Henry Clinton's headquarters before the Battle of Monmouth. The house was built in 1755 and is the oldest residence in Freehold. It is a fine example of pre-Revolutionary crafts-manship and has recently been restored by the Monmouth County Historical Association. A crude painting of a naval scene, above the fireplace in the great bedchamber, has been attributed to a Hessian soldier. Photo courtesy of Samuel Stelle Smith

The Battle of Monmouth is sometimes referred to as the Battle of Monmouth Court House. The courthouse shown was constructed in 1731 to replace one built in 1715; it was replaced in 1809. This painting is one of several of the courthouse by Carrie Swift of Freehold. Photo courtesy of Samuel Stelle Smith

The Tennent Parsonage farmhouse was one of the buildings that stood on the field during the Battle of Monmouth. This wood engraving was made in 1857, two years before the building was demolished because it was in ruin. The farmhouse probably stood on the north side of present state highway 522 and east of the 522 crossing of Weamaconk Creek. Photo courtesy of Samuel Stelle Smith

Saint Peter's Episcopal Church, at 33 Throckmorton Street in Freehold, is considered the oldest church in use in New Jersey. Scottish and English Quakers built the original structure in 1683 at Topanemus, four miles north of Freehold. Saint Peter's was moved south to Freehold, changing its denomination (but not its congregation) en route. The British used the church as a hospital at the Battle of Monmouth; at other times the Americans used it as a barracks and ammunition station. The white-shingled, two-story structure has a small, graceful belfry above the front gable. It has been extensively altered. Photo courtesy of Samuel Stelle Smith

31

Saint Peter's Episcopal Church, Freehold, is shown as it appeared in the 1940s. Photo courtesy of the Monmouth County Historical Association

THE OLD TENNENT CHURCH.

The Old Tennent Church on Gordon's Road in Tennent was erected in 1751; the adjacent cemetery dates to 1731. It is an exceedingly fine example of rural church architecture, and its setting on a low hill, surrounded by an almost endless panorama of ancient gravestones, is memorable. Many of the stones date from the Battle of Monmouth. Lieutenant Colonel Henry Monckton, who was in command of the British Second Grenadiers, is buried here. Photo courtesy of Samuel Stelle Smith

Among Monmouth County's many links with the past is the Witlock-Seabrook homestead, known also as the "Spy House." This historic site, which stands on the dunes of Raritan Bay in Port Monmouth, is now the Shoal Harbor Marine Museum. A house of many generations, it is actually in three sections, with the oldest portion dating back to about 1664. The Spy House title dates back to the Revolution when the British thought the owners, occupying the only house on the beach, were checking on their ships. The house is on the National Register of Historic Sites. Photo courtesy the *Register*

In 1903 the 125th anniversary of the Battle of Monmouth was celebrated in front of the battle monument on Court Street in Freehold. Photo courtesy of the Freehold Borough Library

This statue of *Liberty Triumphant* caps the Monmouth Battle Monument. The monument is on Court Street in Freehold, set on a half-acre wedge of lawn. The ninety-four-foot shaft was designed by Emelin T. Littell and Douglas Smythe. The cornerstone was laid in 1878 on the 100th anniversary of the battle; six years later the monument was unveiled. Photo courtesy of the Monmouth County Historical Association

Monmouth Battlefield State Park, encompassing 1,520 acres, opened to the public in 1977. The park includes a visitors center where interpretive sound and light exhibits of the battle are shown. The battlefield site was purchased in 1973 under the Green Acres Bond Act. Photo from the collection of R. Van Benthuysen

33

In 1928, the sesquicentennial celebration of the Battle of Monmouth was held in Freehold. During the festivities Joe Humphries, the well known sports announcer (*left*), presented a replica of the famous Molly Pitcher flag to Mayor Peter Runyon. Photo courtesy of the Monmouth County Historical Association

This picture shows the reviewing stand at Freehold Raceway in 1928, as Monmouth County observed the 150th anniversary of the Battle of Monmouth; troops of the New Jersey National Guard are shown marching. Photo courtesy of the Monmouth County Historical Association

Philip Freneau, sailor, scholar, and editor, is best known as the "Poet of the Revolution." Among some of his more popular works are "The Wild Honeysuckle" and "The Indian Burying Ground." A fiery Anti-Federalist, he opposed the aristocratic theories of Adams and Hamilton. He established Monmouth County's first newspaper, the *New Jersey Chronicle*, in 1795. Born in New York, Freneau spent most of his life (1752-1832) at "Mount Pleasant," the family homestead in Matawan. The portrait was painted by John Singleton Copley. Photo courtesy of the Frick Collection

Philip Freneau's grave is on a knoll about 100 yards southeast of his boyhood home, Mount Pleasant Hall in Matawan; his mother, Agnes Watson Freneau Kearny, is buried beside him. The grave site is now surrounded by modern split-level homes, but one may see the hills of the Navesink in the distance. Photo from the collection of R. Van Benthuysen

James T. Raleigh of Colts Neck is shown speaking at the dedication of a nineteen-foot wooden beacon that he and several others constructed to commemorate the bicentennial of the American Revolution. Beacons of this type were used in the Revolutionary War for signalling purposes. Three were located in Monmouth County, and twenty others throughout the state of New Jersey. This beacon is located in Holmdel near the intersection of state highway 34 and route 520. Photo courtesy of James T. Raleigh

35

This wooden dwelling has overlooked the creek in Matawan since colonial days when the neighborhood was lively with the bustle of commerce; warehouses and docks were situated here for the sloops which carried Monmouth County produce to New York and Brooklyn. Originally the home of Samuel Forman and his wife Helen Denise, this private home is called the "Old Hospital" because of its use during the Revolutionary War. A skirmish between the Tories and the Continentals took place in the neighborhood, and the wounded were brought to the Forman home. The Formans raised four sons, all officers in the Continental Army, and three daughters. The third daughter Eleanor, married Philip Freneau. Courtesy of the Monmouth College Library

The Allen House, one of Monmouth County's earliest houses, was built about 1670 and makes part of historic Shrewsbury's four corners. It is owned by the Monmouth County Historical Association. The structure is two and one-half stories, with a gambrel roof, interior and exterior end chimneys, and off-center entrance.

A skirmish between the local militia and British troops took place near the house in 1779. In this photograph the house is shown before restoration; the right portion, which was a later addition, has been removed. Photo courtesy of the Shrewsbury Historical Society

36

A well known Monmouth County landmark is Christ Episcopal Church on Broad Street and Sycamore Avenue in Shrewsbury. The parish is one of the oldest in America, having been founded in 1702. The present building was erected in 1769, replacing an earlier stone structure dating from 1715. It was enlarged in 1844.

The church received its charter from King George II on June 3, 1736, and housed Colonial soldiers during the Revolution. It is the mother church of several shore Episcopal parishes. Photo courtesy of the Shrewsbury Historical Society

Colonel Abraham Orsborn, one of the largest landholders in the Brielle area, farmed over 1,000 acres. He had four sons and three daughters. His son, Captain Samuel Orsborn received a parcel of the land upon which this fine home was built. It was typical of the homes of the colonial period, with heavy beams and simple woodwork.

The house was spared from the Tory raid during the Revolution. Today the Manasquan River Golf Club has added to the farmhouse, and the original portion serves as the ladies locker room. Courtesy of the Monmouth College Library

The Seventh Day Adventists from New England who settled in the area of Manasquan and Shark River organized in 1745. The land for their meeting-house was given in 1775 by Zebulon Maxon. Constructed of white oak in 1776, the structure was called the Shrewsbury Church, and had the dimensions of thirty feet by twenty-five feet. When it was sold in 1789, many of the congregation moved to West Virginia. The church was turned, moved, rebuilt, and restored over the years. The congregations were Free Methodists, Baptists, and Universalists. In 1941 it became a Bible Protestant Church, and a new facility was built. Eighteen years ago, the Bible Protestant congregation tried to sell the structure, but it was torn down when a buyer could not be found. The bell was salvaged but none of the beautiful woodwork. The original prerevolutionary churchyard is said to be under the Garden State Parkway. Courtesy of the Monmouth College Library

37

The original owner of this wooden structure in Rumson was William Bingham of Philadelphia, a wealthy merchant and later a Pennsylvania senator. He built this home in 1791, and in its rooms the elite of the period gathered. Senator Bingham's daughter married Lord Ashburton here.

The house was the site of the Bellevue Academy in 1831. Later, Dr. Eleazar Parmly, a renowned dentist, bought the mansion and remodeled it. Bingham Hall remained in the family for generations. Legend has it that the British troops retreating from the heat of the Battle of Monmouth drank the well dry. They must have been lost as well as thirsty and beaten. Courtesy of the Monmouth College Library

This picture shows the Sandy Hook Lighthouse with its original illumination and ventilators on the dome, with stays to assist in cleaning the lantern panes. The lighthouse had a general overhaul in the mid-1800s, but no structural changes were made. Thus, Sandy Hook Lighthouse, from the ground to the light, is today almost exactly as it was when first "fired" nearly 220 years ago. Illustration from the *New York Magazine,* August, 1790; courtesy of Samuel Stelle Smith

Fenwick Lyell (1767-1822) and his brother John (ca. 1769-1811) made furniture in Middletown. In 1798 Fenwick advertised in the *New York Gazette* that he kept a warehouse on Beaver Street where he sold furniture. Photo courtesy of the Monmouth County Historical Association

38

The Joshua Huddy memorial at the Colts Neck Town Hall was dedicated in 1977. The Battle of Monmouth Fife and Drum Corps, the Joshua Huddy Boys' Fife and Drum Corps, and the Freehold Volunteers Fife and Drum Corps participated in the ceremony. Photo Courtesy of the *Register*

The engraving shows Joshua Huddy's house in Colts Neck as it looked in the 1840s; at this time the house was owned by Thomas G. Haight. Photo from Barber and Howe's *Historical Collections of the State of New Jersey*

The Colts Neck Inn is pictured at the turn of the century. The inn is on the north side of the Freehold-Eatontown Highway (present-day state highway 537). It was constructed in 1717 and is still in use; it is currently being remodeled. Photo courtesy of the Freehold Borough Library

The Colts Neck Inn is shown as it looks today. Photo from the collection of R. Van Benthuysen

In the Chapel Hill section of
Middletown, on the King's Highway,
stands a private home originally built
as a Baptist church and meetinghouse
around 1809. This structure was
purchased in 1829 by the Methodist
Episcopal Church for use until the
completion of their new church in
Navesink. The building was then sold
to a Baptist deacon, used occasionally
for services by the Middletown Baptist
Church, and later used by the First
Baptist Church of Middletown. The
High Point Temperance Society held
meetings here. (Chapel Hill prior to
1800 was called High Point.) Courtesy

chapter 4

Country On The Move: 1801-1865

The Old First Methodist Church, in West Long Branch, stands as a landmark of shore Methodism. The first Methodist gatherings were held in the area in 1774. The Reverend Francis Asbury, first Methodist Bishop in America, preached in the vicinity in the year 1785. Construction of the church was started in 1809 and completed in 1819. Interior renovations have been undertaken from time to time, but the exterior is little changed from the earliest days. Photo from the collection of R. Van Benthuysen

By the end of the eighteenth century Monmouth County had passed through its infancy. In the interior, farms had been carved out of the forest and scrub pine, villages had been established, trade and industry had begun, and various religious denominations had firm foundations. Monmouth County had weathered the hardships of the Revolutionary War, and by 1800 it faced a new era. The rich fertile soil, favored by a mild climate, made the area ideal for farming. A ready market for the farmer's products was provided by New York City, located only forty-five miles to the north. The waterways furnished an easy means of transporting fruit and vegetables to the New York market.

The principal sources of the prosperity of Red Bank, declared an account written in 1844, "is the trade with New York. Thirteen sloops and schooners sail from here with vegetables, wood, and oysters for that market, and a steamboat plies regularly between here and the city. Vessels week after week have taken oysters to New York and returned with $600 or $700 for their cargoes."

In the War of 1812 with Great Britain, a number of military companies under Monmouth County officers, and made up of Monmouth men, entered the service. Their principal duties were to guard the coast of the ocean and bays bordering the county. The terms of service were brief, averaging less than three months. Most of the Monmouth County troops were not called on to take part in any operation against the enemy. However, the presence of British naval vessels patrolling off the coast subjected the residents to a feeling of the immediacy of war.

One defense group stationed near Shark River did encounter the enemy. On April 2, 1814 this band was patrolling the coast; they had six field pieces and 100 muskets. Their day of glory came when they drove off a small British warship which had bombarded and attempted to destroy shipping in the Shark River.

In writing of Monmouth County's industrial history, the starting point is James Grover's establishment of the first bog iron furnace, at Tinton Falls near Shrewsbury, in 1664. However, the largest and best-known ironworks in the county was that operated by James P. Allaire, a New York brass founder who purchased the Monmouth Furnace in 1822. He changed the name to the Howell Works and set up a self-sustaining village. By 1840 Allaire's facility had become the largest iron furnace in the young nation. At the peak of his fortune, Allaire's realm of 11,000 acres had probably 500 employees and seventy buildings. Ten of the latter are still standing, including the beehive furnace stack. Dependent on bog iron and charcoal, Allaire's village began to decline about 1846 when hardrock iron ore and anthracite were discovered side by side in Pennsylvania.

Today the deserted village of Allaire stands in a quiet unspoiled section of Monmouth County as a silent reminder of the bog iron industry of bygone days. Allaire is significant in our industrial history because most of the buildings used during its heyday as an operating furnace are still standing. Over the past two decades the village has undergone a major restoration and is now part of the New Jersey State Park System.

During the second quarter of the nineteenth century Monmouth County became the home of a unique experiment in communal living which lasted twelve years. There were a number of socialistic communities established in the nation during this period. One of the best known was Brook Farm in West Roxbury, Massachusetts. The Monmouth County community-living project, begun in 1843, was located in Colts Neck and was called the North American Phalanx. Among its many distinctions was that it marketed the first boxed cereal in the nation.

The North American Phalanx was born from the ideas of Charles Fourier of France, who developed a plan for social reorganization. People would live away from major cities, in groups of 400 to 4,000 to be known as phalanxes.

This wooden meetinghouse stands fenced among old oaks on busy Route 35 in Manasquan. It was built by the Society of Friends in the late nineteenth century upon the site of an earlier building. The gravestones in its cemetery date from 1811. Courtesy of the Monmouth College Library

The phalanxes would be self-supporting, grow their own food, and make their own clothes, furniture, and other articles. The inhabitants would be housed in huge hotel-like buildings called phalansteries.

By 1852 the North American Phalanx was one of the most productive farms in New Jersey. It began to sell its surplus products to outsiders, transporting them by steamboat from Red Bank and Keyport to New York. Food stamped N.A.P. was of excellent quality and eagerly sought by dealers.

The colony was weakened in 1853 when several members withdrew to form the Raritan Bay Union at Perth Amboy, New Jersey. Then in 1854 a fire destroyed the flour mill, the sawmill, the smithy, and some valuable machinery. These two events signaled the end of the colony. During its history the North American Phalanx had several significant achievements: profit-sharing, the thirty-hour week,

44

The Shrewsbury Presbyterian Church stands among the group of old houses of worship that grace the quaint corner of this historic borough. The congregation dates back to 1727, but the present church was built in 1821. It is a good example of the plain lines of architecture that found favor with the stern settlers of Monmouth County. This photograph was taken about 1880. Photo courtesy of the Shrewsbury Historical Society

planned recreation for workers, religious toleration, and profitable industries.

While the residents of the mainland villages enjoyed beach parties and bathing in the surf, they were well aware that the very breakers which offered them pleasure could be the cause of widespread destruction. Shipwrecks were the most dramatic demonstrations of man's struggle against nature. They occurred mainly in the fall and winter months.

The first lighthouse in Monmouth County had been built on Sandy Hook as early as 1761 by New York merchants. However, it became recognized that some kind of responsible rescue service, subsidized by the federal government, should be established. The first kind of aid to come from Congress was the establishment of a series of lighthouses. In 1828 the federal government began by constructing Highland Light on the Navesink Highlands.

While the construction of lighthouses helped to reduce the number of wrecks, there were still disasters, and the development of lifesaving stations helped to save crews and passengers on the foundered vessels. The assumption of federal responsibility in this service may be credited to William Augustus Newell, a Monmouth County physician who practiced in Allentown. On August 13, 1839, Dr. Newell stood on the beach at Long Beach Island and watched thirteen men of the grounded Austrian brig, the *Count Perasto,* perish as they tried to swim a mere three hundred yards to safety. The doctor's quick mind figured that it ought to be possible to shoot a line from a shortened musket across a stranded ship; that line, in turn, could be used to pull a heavy rope to the stricken vessel.

Newell was later elected to Congress and served two terms as a Whig, from 1847 to 1851. In 1848 he pushed through an appropriation of $10,000 for lifesaving stations on the East Coast. The first such station, complete with Dr. Newell's lifeline invention, was built on Sandy Hook. That tiny building still exists today, although it has been moved to Twin Lights on the Highlands of the Navesink.

Present-day Ocean County was set off from Monmouth County in 1850. Transportation problems made the residents of the area favor separation. It was difficult to get to the county seat at Freehold for meetings of the county court and for the recording of deeds, as well as for looking up titles to land records.

Despite the fact that the county was not invaded, as it had been during the Revolutionary War, the Civil War seriously affected the lives of all county residents. Every community sent some sons off to the conflict. The area sent men who took part in various seagoing expeditions,. Skiffs of a special type, constructed in the winter of 1859 by Walter Seaman of Long Branch, were taken on the naval expedition that attacked New Orleans. The boats were used to land soldiers and were forerunners of some of the landing craft used in World War II.

The Fourteenth Volunteer Infantry of New Jersey was one of the state's quota of five regiments required under the call for 300,000 men issued by President Lincoln on July 7, 1862. It was raised and organized at Camp Vredenburgh, near the old Monmouth battleground, a short distance from the village of Freehold. The regiment was mustered into service on August 26, 1862, and left its camp at Freehold, 950 strong, on September 2, 1862. When the unit returned three years later, there were only 230 men remaining. The regiment had traveled by rail 1,051 miles, by water 628 miles, and on foot 2,015 miles. ●

45

The Friends Meeting House in Shrewsbury is located on the northeast corner of Sycamore Avenue and Broad Street; the present house of worship was built in 1816. Photo courtesy of the Shrewsbury Historical Society

The picture shows Matawan's main street about 1840. This area was originally called Middletown Point. When first settled by the Scotch it was called New Aberdeen. Photo from Barber and Howe's *Historical Collections of the State of New Jersey*

This is a view of Middletown in 1844. Photo from Barber and Howe's *Historical Collections of the State of New Jersey*

This is how the Monmouth County Courthouse on Main Street in Freehold appeared in 1840; the building was erected in 1800. Photo from Barber and Howe's *Historical Collections of the State of New Jersey*

This is the historic Shrewsbury intersection, at present-day Route 35 and Sycamore Avenue, as it appeared in the 1840s; on the right is Christ Episcopal Church. Photo from Barber and Howe's *Historical Collections of the State of New Jersey*

This is a view of the Presbyterian
Church in Allentown, erected in 1837;
the congregation was established in
1756. Photo from Barber and Howe's
*Historical Collections of the State of
New Jersey*

The Monmouth County Plank Road
Company was incorporated in 1850 and
built its first road in 1851. Sixty feet
wide, the road connected Matawan, Keyport, Marlboro, and Freehold. A turn-
pike with a stone surface, connecting
Middletown and Holmdel, was laid in
1859. To maintain the roads tolls were
collected for the vehicles and animals
using them. Route 34 follows part of
this roadway. This toll house was
situated on Route 9. Courtesy of the
Matawan-Aberdeen Public Library

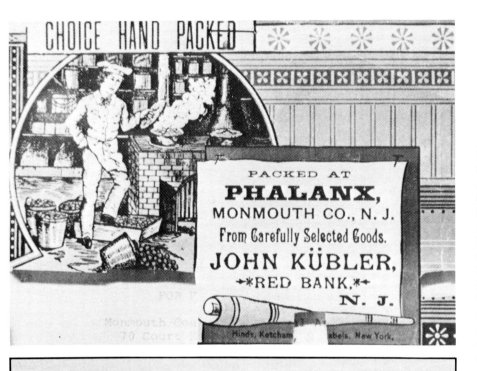

CHOICE HAND PACKED

PACKED AT
PHALANX,
MONMOUTH CO., N. J.
From Carefully Selected Goods.
JOHN KÜBLER,
＊RED BANK.＊
N. J.

Hinds, Ketcham, Label, New York.

Many canners and packers produced and marketed fruit and vegetables. Among the most interesting were those packed by organizations in the Phalanx area, a center of industry for many years. The North American Phalanx, five miles west of Red Bank, was started by disciples of Fourier. The local society consisted of about fifty families, many from the Albany, New York area. They and their families resided in a three-story building; operated sawmills, grist mills, and wood shops; and provided a school for the community's children. A disastrous fire and personal friction caused the dispersal of the group. The first boxed cereal originated at the North American Phalanx. Courtesy of the *Register*

Positive Sale

OF THE

DOMAIN OF THE PHALANX.

THE NORTH AMERICAN PHALANX OFFERS FOR SALE ITS ENTIRE ESTATE, REAL AND MOVABLE:

The domain contains nearly seven hundred acres, comprising a diversity of soil in good culture, of easy tillage, and having extensive improvements and great natural advantages and resources such as arable uplands (upon which there have been distributed within the last twelve years about 40,000 tons of marl), about 315 acres exceedingly well adapted to Farming, Market Gardening and Fruit Culture; natural meadow, from which two crops a year are cut, about 70 acres; woodlands, well timbered with oak, hickory, chestnut, locust (native and cultivated groves), about 220 acres; orchards, comprising the usual variety and succession of peaches, some seventy varieties of the choicest apples (trees of remarkable thrift and vigor, four to twelve years' growth, the older ones bearing quite freely); pears, standard and on quince stocks; plumbs, nectarines, quince, grapes, &c., all bountifully watered by springs and brooks, together with extensive marl beds (Hop Brook, and Dry Bank); buildings, comprising a large central edifice with large dining-room, kitchen, laundry with steam engine, dairy, ice-house, and all the appointments of a complete Establishment, lodgings and separate tenements, outhouses, a large brick building (40x75 feet, two and a half stories, with cement cellar floor) for agricultural purposes, and fitted up with apparatus for preserving and drying fruits and vegetables. All these have water distributed through them, supplied from never failing springs by force-pump and water-wheel. The whole Establishment is admirably adapted to and prepared for the use of an Association, or for an Agricultural College.

The Estate will be sold together or in parcels to suit purchasers. If divided it will be into about forty separate parcels, fairly distributing the natural advantages and improvements, and offering great inducements to Farmers, Market Gardeners, Artizans; also (with the central buildings) as a place for Water-Cure, a Boarding-School, a Summer Boarding-House, or an Agricultural College, the advantages are very great.

The plan of division adopted is as follows : See Map.

CLASS I. Parcels 1 to 14, Buildings, Building Lots, &c.
No. 1—The CENTRAL BUILDINGS, GROUNDS and appurtenances.
The buildings are
a. The PRINCIPAL EDIFICE comprising Main Section, Rear Section, and East Wing.
The Main Section besides a cellar has on the
First Floor.—Office, reading room, parlor and bed-room.
Second Floor.—Two tenements, and three bed-rooms.
Third Floor.—Six lodging rooms.
The REAR SECTION contains, Cellar, Store room, Dairy (with cement floor,) Kitchen, Pastry room, small Dining Room, Boiler and Engine, (for cooking, washing, churning, sawing wood &c.) Laundry (two floors,) main dining Room (70x29 ft. and 15 ft. between floors) and fifteen Lodging rooms.
The EAST WING comprises Four tenements, two stories, 22 to 26 ft. front, and 29 feet deep, with cellars and front and rear piazzas.

b. DWELLING HOUSE.—40x80 ft. two stories, with dormer windows, and containing 23 tenements and lodgings.
c. The old Homestead with cribs and sheds.
TOGETHER with about FIFTEEN ACRES of LAND, comprising Lawns, Groves, Lakelet, Hydraulic works (carrying water through all the principal buildings), vines, ornamental trees &c.
Nos. 2 to 9.—are COTTAGE LOTS, containing about an acre each, and pleasantly located on the same table as the Central Buildings.
No. 10.—ASPARAGUS LOT near Main Edifice, and contains about seven-eighths of an acre.
No. 11. OUT HOUSES. Barn, cow stable, ox barn and shed, and about one and an eighth acres of Land, supplied with water from Hydraulic works.
Nos. 12 to 14.—THREE GARDEN BUILDING LOTS, containing about an acre each.
CLASS II. Comprising eight or ten Garden Plots, of 5 to 14 acres each, of mellow loam and contiguous to the marl beds.
No. 14.—GARDEN PLOT containing about six and five eighths acres, part of which is planted with vines and other fruit, part with osier, asparagus beds &c. The remainder is in garden culture and pond.
No. 16.—KITCHEN GARDEN. Rear of Main Edifice, contains about four and one sixth acres, part of which is in asparagus beds, small fruit &c., and the remainder in garden culture.
No. 17.—MILL LOT. Containing nearly six acres, part cleared part wood land and part meadow on Trout Brook; and having a carpenter shop, two stories, 30x40, three sides of lower story filled in with brick, affording room for shop and dwelling.
No. 18.—The MARKET HOUSE, or Seristery Lot. Containing over thirteen and a half acres of desirable Garden Land, upon which is the substantial Brick Building 40x75 ft. two and a half stories, with cement cellar floor under the entire building; having apparatus with steam boiler, vats, enameled pans, &c., for preserving, and putting up fresh fruits and vegetables; a large drying closet with hot air chamber, in which fruit, okra, green corn &c., can be thoroughly dried in a few hours; vats for washing vegetables for market; ample store room, and supply of water from Hydraulic works.
Nos. 19 to 25.—FOUR GARDEN PLOTS, containing five and a quarter acres each; one of ten and a half acres; one of thirteen and a half acres; one of fourteen and a half, and one of twenty one and a half acres; all of which are very desirable EARLY GARDEN LANDS, and most of them have portions of wood or locust grove.
CLASS III. Comprising ten Farms, containing 20 to 80 acres each, and having due shares of upland, meadow, wood land, water, &c.
No. 26.—PEAR ORCHARD FARM, containing about fifty-two acres of excellent loam, of which over thirty-five acres are in grass

This poster announces the sale of the North American Phalanx. The unique experiment in communal living flourished from 1843 to 1855. The old Van Mater farm in Colts Neck, purchased for $8,000 in 1843, was the site of the Phalanx. Although the community prospered, an undercurrent of disagreement began to develop, fostered by a desire for personal gain. Other rifts slowly destroyed the religious tolerance that had been a cornerstone of the community. A destructive fire destroyed most of the buildings in 1854, and the members could not agree on rebuilding the mills. The lone remaining building was destroyed by fire in the early 1970s. Photo courtesy of the Monmouth College Library

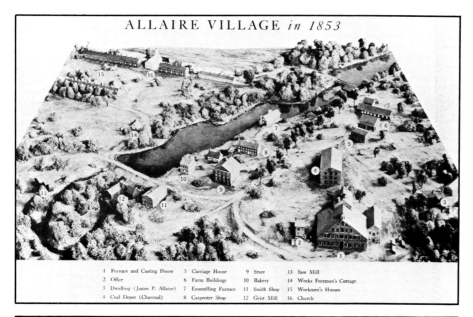

ALLAIRE VILLAGE *in 1853*

1 Furnace and Casting House	5 Carriage House	9 Store	13 Saw Mill
2 Office	6 Farm Buildings	10 Bakery	14 Works Foreman's Cottage
3 Dwelling (James P. Allaire)	7 Enamelling Furnace	11 Smith Shop	15 Workmen's Houses
4 Coal Depot (Charcoal)	8 Carpenter Shop	12 Grist Mill	16 Church

Allaire Village, employing about 500 "hands," was a celebrated "bog iron" furnace and forge located on the New Jersey coastal plain. In its heyday in 1850 Allaire was a self-contained community complete with general store, bakery, church, and school. Here were made caldrons, pots, kettles, bake pans, stoves, sewer pipe, and sadirons. Photo courtesy of the Deserted Village at Allaire, Inc.

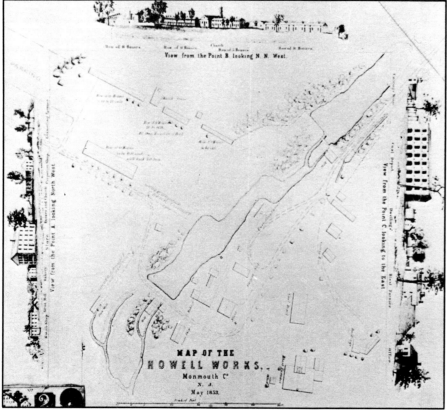

Many of the structures at Allaire have been preserved and are open for visits and other activities. Operated by a volunteer historical group, the entire area is now a state park. Of interest is the well preserved blast furnace, one of the largest during its period of construction. Courtesy of the Newark Public Library

The Monmouth Furnace, an ironworks using bog iron, charcoal, and oyster or clam shells for flux was started in the county as early as 1673. It was purchased by James P. Allaire in 1822 and renamed the Howell Works and Howell Iron Furnace. The works were in operation until 1846. Today the site is called the Deserted Village at Allaire and the Allaire Village, named for its last proprietor, James P. Allaire, a New York iron founder. The village was a self-contained community built around the works. The Howell Works and its furnace produced hollowware, locally-used architectural castings, and water pipe, some of which was used in New York City. The 1853 map of the "Howell Works" was used to promote the sale of the closed works. In map and views it depicts the furnace and the entire village, which may have had a population of several hundred at the height of its activity. Courtesy of the Monmouth College Library

50

The Allaire general store was substantially built in 1835 at a cost of $7,000; the store is the largest structure now standing at the village. It is located in the center of the complex. Four stories high and of brick construction, the store was a marvel of its day. Because of the isolated location of the works, an enormous stock was carried and the store was patronized both by Howell employees and by residents from miles around. Photo courtesy of the Monmouth County Historical Association

The Allaire church, originally Episcopal, was built using some timbers from a log raft washed ashore at Manasquan. It was in intermittent use until sometimes after 1900, then closed until its recent restoration. It is unusual in having the tower at the altar end of the building. Courtesy of the Newark Public Library

The Allaire Church was an important center of village activity and continues in operation. It is presently a popular place for summer weddings. Courtesy of the Newark Public Library

51

The first eight lifesaving stations of the U.S. Life Saving Service were unmanned boathouses stocked with rescue apparatus. They were twenty-eight feet long and sixteen feet wide, one-and-a-half stories high, and covered with cedar shingles. The Sandy Hook Station is the sole remaining example of these eight stations. It has been moved from Sandy Hook to the Twin Lights Museum, Highlands. Photo from the collection of R. Van Benthuysen

By 1868 Life-Saving Station No. 4 at Long Branch was one of a network spaced every five miles along the beach. Pictured at the right is Charles H. Green, recipient of a gold medal presented by the New York Life Saving Association for the rescue of the *Adonis* and her crew of eighteen during a March storm in 1859. Courtesy of the Monmouth College Library

The numerous lifesaving stations, like the example at West End, housed surfboats and their crews which were used to render aid in case of shipwreck. They were established through the efforts of a local physician, Dr. William A. Newell, while he was in Congress in 1848. The stations, at short intervals along the coast, had regular foot patrols between stations, and were equipped with breeches buoys and line guns for rescue if they were unable to launch surfboats from the beach. The shore stations were replaced by stations at Sandy Hook; Shark River Inlet; and Manasquan Inlet, which had power surfboats. Courtesy of the Monmouth College Library

52

The breeches buoy was the salvation of the shipwrecked if conditions prevented rescue by surfboat. This unusually well-painted and polished Life Saving Service beach cart carried the necessary equipment. The cart, with large-diameter wheels and wide iron tires could negotiate the beach with relative ease, generally propelled by the crew and occasionally by a team for longer distances.

The equipment consisted of a pair of shear legs, the breeches buoy, blocks, a sand anchor, a Lyle gun to fire the line, and a chest of line. The chest of "faked down" line rode over the rear wheels. The reel underneath carried heavier line which was to be hauled aboard the stricken vessel by means of the lighter line which had been carried by the Lyle gun projectile. The shear legs were erected to keep the heavier line off the beach after the sand anchor secured its beach end. The breeches buoy, a large circular cork life ring with attached canvas "trousers" without feet, was suspended on a large line by a snatch block with a large roller. The breeches buoy was propelled back and forth between the ship and beach by the smaller line, carrying passengers and crew to safety. Courtesy of Moss Archives

The loss of life was occasionally great. This memorial to the passengers of the *New Era* was erected in the cemetery of the Old First Methodist Church in West Long Branch, at the gravesite. In 1854 the ship came ashore near the outlet from Deal Lake between the present Asbury Park and Loch Arbour. Weather conditions made rescue difficult, and 240 German immigrant passengers were lost. Photo courtesy of Charles, Maps, Junior

At the urgings of William Torrey of Eatontown and Woolman Stokes of Long Branch, two of a group of enterprising gentlemen, a spur was run from the main branch of the Raritan and Delaware Bay Railroad Company at Eatontown to Second Avenue and Broadway in Long Branch. On June 18, 1860 the first train pulled into Long Branch. Some denounced the scheme as leading to the ruin of the most favored seashore resort. Courtesy of the Monmouth College Library

The *Monmouth Democrat,* which published its first issue on April 12, 1834, was advertised in this Monmouth County Fair bulletin of 1886. The paper was founded by Bernard Connolly, who backed President Jackson in his opposition to the rechartering of the United States Bank. Connolly used the paper to win support for Jackson. In 1854 the *Democrat* was purchased by James S. Yard. While dedicated to the party and Democratic ideals, the new editor scrutinized the issues. He never lost sight of the fact that the paper was a family newspaper and saw to it that the paper was never overwhelmed with politics. Courtesy of the Monmouth College Library

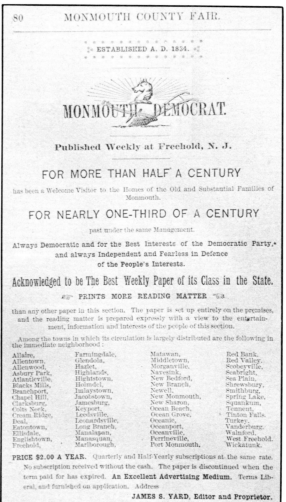

54

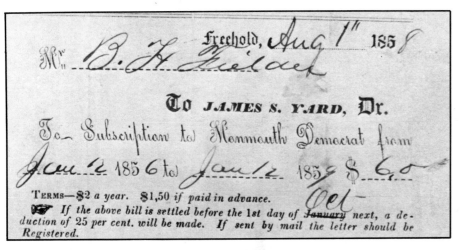

This receipt is for a three-year subscription to the *Monmouth Democrat*. Photo courtesy of the Monmouth College Library

The Neptune Club of New York was built in 1858 on the Navesink River between Upper and Lower Rocky Point. The roof of this one-story wooden structure was built around the trees. The forty associates of the club were members of the Neptune Volunteer Fire Company of New York. Courtesy of the Monmouth College Library

Henry Morford, journalist and author, was born in what was then known as Chanceville (now New Monmouth) on March 10, 1823. He spent most of his youth and early manhood in his native town, first as a merchant and later as postmaster of the village, but his leisure was given to writing verse. In 1852 he established at Middletown Point (now Matawan) a weekly newspaper called the *New Jersey Standard.* He later wrote several novels, among them *The Spur of Monmouth,* whose subject was suggested, no doubt, by the battlefield near which he lived as a boy. Courtesy of the Monmouth College Library

Meerschaum Villa at Park and Norwood avenues, Elberon, was purchased in 1868 by James Hubert McVicker, a well-known actor and Chicago theatrical manager. Edwin Booth was a frequent visitor to the house and can be seen leaning against a post. The child in the hammock was Booth's by his deceased wife. (In 1881 he married his second wife, Mary Frances McVicker.) The villa was sold to the famous stage star, Maggie Mitchell in 1875. Courtesy of the Monmouth College Library

Henry M. Alexander, a prominent member of the bar of New York, built this plain country cottage in 1858. He commissioned E. T. Potter, a New York architect, to design this unpretentious home, which was isolated on the bluff in the Elberon section of Long Branch. In spite of the absence of trees the house was called The Grove. In 1877 the home was sold to George Pullman of Pullman Car fame. Courtesy of the Monmouth College Library

In 1857 Dr. Z. W. Scriven designed his Roman Doric home on Main Streeet (now Broadway) in Long Branch. The doctor, a horticulturist and owner of a farm in Farmingdale, planted orchards and gardens in the rear of this imposing structure. Dr. Scriven was a graduate of Union College, Schenectady, and Albany Medical College. He was a general practitioner, chief surgeon for the vicinity, and an original director of the first railroad to Long Branch. Courtesy of the Monmouth College Library

56

The Rue Pottery Company plant on Main Street in Matawan manufactured majolica and other pottery. Purchased by the Matawan Tile Company in 1902, its tile was used in the Boston subway system and the Rutgers University gymnasium. The Matawan Tile Company went out of business in the early forties, but the building is still being utilized by the Salmon Paper Box Company. Courtesy of the Matawan Aberdeen Public Library

The New Bedford Carriage Shop in Wall Township was also called the Old Horseshoe Foundry. After the Civil War the Morris Brothers built carriages in this sturdy brick building. The property originally belonged to the Allgor-Kittel family who ran a blacksmith, wheelwright establishment. Allgor was a township committee member and the property followed his line. Courtesy of the Monmouth College Library

There were many early schools in the Freehold vicinity; Allentown was a school center. The children of this small farm community once attended the grade school shown here. This photograph was taken in 1911. Today Allentown's elementary children attend the Upper Freehold Regional Elementary School on High Street. Courtesy of the Moss Archives

Long Branch first became established as a summer resort in the latter part of the eighteenth century. However, it was not until the 1850s that it began to attract large numbers of visitors. An indication of the popularity of the resort may become apparent from the number of illustrations that appeared in national magazines such as *Harper's Weekly* and *Frank Leslie's Illustrated Newspaper* highlighting the attractions of "The Branch." Photo courtesy of the Durnell Collection, Monmouth College Library

Guests came from New York by steamboat, train, and stagecoach to spend the summer at the Little Silver boardinghouse at the end of Little Silver Point Road. The guest house was owned and managed in the early years by the Pontin family. Courtesy of the Monmouth College Library

58

Several boat lines carried passengers and freight between New York City and the towns along the Shrewsbury and Navesink rivers. Service extended as far as Red Bank and North Long Branch by different lines, some stopping en route. The *Albertina* and the *Seabird* provided pleasant service to Red Bank and other towns on the Shrewsbury. Courtesy of the Monmouth College Library

59

In 1853 Monmouth County's first railroad was in full operation. For years before it became a reality, public meetings and newspaper articles had focused attention on Monmouth County's need for rail transportation as the farmers and businessmen pressed for its construction. Interested parties fought hard for three years to get a bill through the legislature, and by 1851 the Freehold and Jamesburg Agricultural Railroad Company was formed. At a cost of $220,666, in 1853 the company built tracks eleven and a half miles long between Freehold and the mainline at Jamesburg. The 1857 invoice at right lists pork, cheese, coffee, candles, and other merchandise shipped by the railroad to Mr. A. D. Havens from New York. Courtesy of the Monmouth College Library

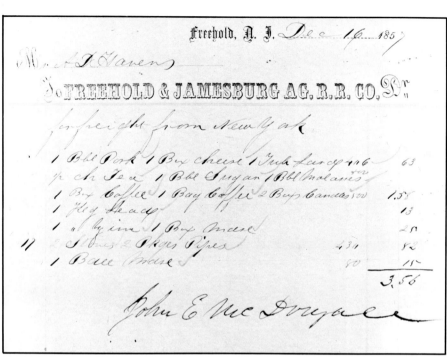

Historic Twin Lights in Highlands served in days past to guide mariners safely to New York and New Jersey harbors. Built in 1862, Twin Lights was designated a national landmark by the U.S. Department of the Interior in 1965, and is now a museum. It was from the site of Twin Lights that the first wigwag signals were sent by

General Albert J. Myer from Highlands to Fort Hamilton, New York. The wigwag system worked so well it formed the basis for future systems used during the Civil War and for the establishment of the first Signal Corps by the U.S. Army in 1863. Photo courtesy of the Monmouth College Library

60

James Gordon Bennett, the publisher and editor of the *New York Herald,* supported the South, secession, and Douglas. Here he is seen on August 22, 1861, welcoming Mrs. Lincoln to Long Branch where a ball is to be held in her honor. Contemporary papers were filled with news of the arrangements and appointments for the affair which eclipsed all previous "hops" at this favorite watering place. The Long Branch hotels swelled with guests and every cot and other hotel contrivance was brought into play for the comfort of the guests. A storm prevented the "country people" from assembling in great throngs. "To the great credit of the villagers it should be said that their curiosity was not obtrusive . . . ." Mrs. Lincoln appeared at ten and retired at midnight. The merriment continued until three in the morning. Courtesy of the Monmouth College Library

Joel Parker was born in Freehold in November 1816. His father was sheriff of Monmouth County, a member of the assembly, state treasurer, and state librarian. The young Parker, a Princeton graduate, studied law in the office of Henry W. Green in Trenton. After admittance to the bar Parker returned to Freehold to practice. Parker's election to the assembly in 1847 began his public career which culminated in his post as governor of New Jersey in 1863. Photo from the collection of R. Van Benthuysen

61

Mrs. Abraham Lincoln, when she visited Long Branch during the first summer of the Civil War, chose to stay at the Mansion House, then the city's finest hotel. President Grant, during his first summer in Long Branch in 1869, also stayed at the Mansion House for a brief period. In his *Book of Summer Resorts,* published in 1868, Charles R. Sweetster rated the local hotels accordingly: "Howland's is the most exclusive, Stetson's the most elegant, the Continental the largest and gayest, the Mansion House the finest situated for the water and the Metropolitan the nearest to the cars and the most reasonable in price." Photo courtesy of the Monmouth College Library

The illustration shows scenes on the beach at Long Branch on the Fourth of July, 1863. The bathers in the drawings have a variety of expressions. The center illustration shows the bluff as it was at Long Branch in the 1860s. Illustration from *Harper's Weekly,* 1863

62

The Sandy Hook Lightship guarded the entrance to New York Harbor for many years; within the past decade it has been replaced by a permanent platform. Illustration from *Harper's New Monthly Magazine,* March 1869

Sandy Hook, N.J.

News of arriving vessels and their cargoes was vital to shippers and merchants. The vantage points of Sandy Hook or the Highlands of the Navesink permitted early recognition of vessels entering New York harbor by a margin of hours. Originally transmitted by semaphore system, data was more reliably forwarded by telegraph. The Western Union and Postal Telegraph towers are shown here. Courtesy of the Moss Archives.

chapter 5

Monmouth County Learns To Play: 1866~1900

It is said that the resort industry began in 1790 when Lewis McKnight purchased 100 acres of land in Long Branch for 700 pounds and opened the first "tavern house" for vacationers; members of the best Philadelphia families were his guests. Advertisements extolling the grandeur of a seashore resort in Shrewsbury were printed in a Philadelphia newspaper in 1793. In those days travel to watering places was by private carriage; the vacationers journeyed from Philadelphia, Trenton, and Princeton. In 1840 one steamer left New York and deposited travelers in Sea Bright where they boarded stages for Long Branch. The seaside resort was discovered by the wealthy New Yorkers around 1850; huge hotels were constructed and beautiful summer cottages dotted the shoreline.

Although rail lines went to other parts of the state, and an agricultural railroad ran from Freehold to Keyport, the first excursionists did not arrive in Long Branch by train until 1860. After the Civil War, Monmouth County and New York

were linked with the chartering of the New York and Long Branch Railroad. Another line was built in 1863 which followed the shoreline north, terminating at the New York steamer dock at Sandy Hook. By the turn of the century a railroad network with other shore points had developed. Nearly every town had its own depot; the train stopped at towns whose names have disappeared from today's maps—Normandie, Low Moor, Galilee, Lake Como, Ocean Beach, and Brighton.

After the Civil War, President Ulysses S. Grant summered in Long Branch, and his presence attracted others. George W. Childs, William E. Drexel, and John Hoey erected palatial homes. Colonel Jim Fisk and his entourage of hangers-on were frequent visitors. Stage luminaries Edwin Booth, Lester Wallack, Olive Dowd Byron, and Maggie Mitchell were residents. Lily Langtry dazzled the community with her fine horses and carriage during the afternoon driving hour.

Hotels rivalled Saratoga and Newport. Gambling emporiums lured the plungers to roulette, faro, and poker. Monmouth County, famous since earliest times for horse breeding, became the nation's sports center. Until the antigambling legis-

lation of 1894, followers of the nags and the cream of society frequented the meets at Monmouth Park, a one-mile track. President Grant watched the sport from his box procured for the season.

To the south of Long Branch the town of Ocean Grove was founded in 1868 by William B. Osborn, son of a Methodist minister. Chosen originally as a site for a revival meeting, the enterprise boomed into camp meetings which were held the last ten days of August. The visitors, abjuring materialism and embracing temperance in all things, flocked to the meetings, staying the time in tents. The town was plotted out in 1870, and by 1872 there were 300 cottages in this experimental community. With the advent of the railroad in 1875, the town burgeoned, and its appearance changed to that of a summer community. In contrast to the lavish structures further north, simple Victorian cottages were built. The most conspicuous structure, the Auditorium, was dedicated in 1894 and today is still the heart of the community. This building holds between 8,000 and 9,000 people. Eminent artists have performed and speakers have lectured here; the summer programs continue.

The first lot owner in Ocean

Grove, James Bradley, was determined to start a resort of his own. Between 1872 and 1877 he organized and plotted the acreage north of Ocean Grove (reached by ferry) and named it Asbury Park for the first bishop of the Methodist Church in America. By the turn of the century more than one million pleasure seekers visited Asbury Park each summer. The high standards of the town as a family resort—the piers, promenades, children's carnivals, water pageants, baby parades, its accessibility to the family of moderate means—helped Asbury Park gain the title of "gem" of the Monmouth County shore.

Further to the south the formation of new towns followed a pattern. One or more businessmen formed a land association, purchased farm acreage which was divided into lots, and petitioned the legislature for a public road to be built. Then a large grand hotel was financed. Belmar, Spring Lake, Sea Girt, and Atlantic Highlands to the north are a result of such entrepreneurial vigor.

Inland, away from the hurdy-gurdy of the shoreline, the inhabitants followed their pastoral occupations, living less frenetic lives. The larger townships boasted newspapers and private academies,

66

This dramatic scene shows a ship aground on the north Jersey coast in the 1860s. In the foreground a life-saving crew prepares to launch its boat in a rescue attempt. To the left, a team of men shoot a mortar with a line attached, to the foundering vessel. Illustration from *Harper's New Monthly Magazine,* March 1869

banks, and fire companies. Most towns had post offices, hotels and taverns, drugstores, saddle and harness shops, livery stables, churches and lodges. Roads crisscrossed the county.

In spite of the hostility and protestations of the townspeople, railroads were charted through or near the towns. They were good for business. The railroads brought the excursionists and hauled the marl which had been discovered in Farmingdale (increasing the productivity of the farmers). They moved otherwise perishable produce to market, and those who made their livelihoods from the sea depended on the rails to preserve the freshness of their fish and shellfish.

The prosperous town of Red Bank, linked with New York by water trade since the early days, manufactured furniture, hats, and window sashes. The Navesink River also provided great summer and winter sports—iceboating, sailing, crabbing, and fishing.

The courthouse in Freehold was the center of activity for the county. Freehold had the air and bustle of a city about its work of government, and the landscape of a sleepy agricultural community.

Toward the end of the nineteenth century railways or trolleys also

linked the towns. Originally pulled by horses or mules, the streetcars were electrified with the advent of street electricity.

Monmouth County was stepping into the twentieth century. ●

Talented illustrator, competent painter, and muralist, John W. Alexander captured a special moment on the beach at Sea Bright. Pausing beside a background of beached boats, hardy fishermen and fashionable couples heard, rising above the soft sounds of the sea, a Sunday morning sermon eloquently delivered by a visiting minister from New York. Illustration from *Harper's Weekly,* September 3, 1887

Curlew Hotel, Allenhurst, N. J.

2298

Many of the shore resort towns had large summer hotels, particularly Long Branch, Asbury Park, Ocean Grove, and Spring Lake. Other communities were less well-known, but had hotels with well established reputations and loyal clienteles. Examples were the Octagon at Sea Bright and the Curlew at Allenhurst. Courtesy of the Monmouth College Library

The Globe Hotel, a three-and-one-half story wooden structure on Front Street in Red Bank, was a stage stop and the center for weddings, balls, horse trading, drinking, and gossip. Captain's chairs lined the porch, which ran the full length of the building; politics, the weather, and crops were discussed from this vantage point while the comings and goings of visitors and townfolk were noted. Large stables were built behind the hotel to accommodate travelers and visitors. Courtesy of the Monmouth College Library

Though this picture was taken in 1915, it is typical of the tent lifestyle at the Methodist camp of Ocean Grove which has existed from 1868 to the present. The tent colony around Auditorium Square folds and the vacationers head for home after the Labor Day weekend. Year after year many return, some not Methodists, or even Christians, to summer in the tents. They are a reminder of the days of the early camp meetings when the first prayer meeting was held in a candlelit tent. Constructed of a combination of canvas and wood, the tents are more spacious and homey than one might suppose. The bedroom-living room portion is under the canvas roof; the kitchen and bathroom in the rear are under the permanent wooden structure. Courtesy of the Monmouth College Library

This cartman worked out of the Adams Express Company office near the Asbury Park railroad station. Here he is seen delivering trunks to residents who would be staying in Ocean Grove for the summer. The company gave the same service in Long Branch; the Adams Express Company business was located on Ocean Avenue, near Broadway. Courtesy of the Moss Archives

Before 1889 Belmar was called Ocean Beach. Then it became Elcho in 1889, and Belmar in 1893. The 400 acres between Avon-by-the-Sea and Spring Lake were well suited to a resort, fronting on the ocean and having river-front lots on the Shark River. The Ocean Beach Association was incorporated on March 12, 1872 by a group of Ocean Grove summer residents who felt that Ocean Grove was becoming too crowded. The Belmar Inn was typical of the smaller boarding houses and hotels in the smaller shore towns. Courtesy of the Moss Archives

In celebration of the centennial of Ocean Grove, in 1969, this house at the corner of Central Avenue and McClintock Street was restored and repainted in the original colors. Mrs. Robert Skold donated the cottage to be used as a living history museum. Courtesy of Jane Grammer

70

The pioneer lumbermen of Ocean Grove and Asbury park were G. V. Smock and N. E. Buchanon; their yard was located on the corner of Main and Asbury avenues in Asbury Park. Much of the early building material for resort hotels and homes in Asbury Park and Ocean Grove was supplied by Smock and Buchanon. The firm went out of business in about 1980. Photo from the *Historical and Biographical Atlas of the New Jersey Coast, 1879*

In 1866 Thomas S. R. Brown, who had been an apprentice mason and builder in his youth, opened a hardware, coal, and lumber business in Keyport. Brown was influential in the development of the town and in the area as one of the incorporators of the First National Bank of Keyport and as president of the Middletown Point and Keyport Gas Company. In 1866 Brown was elected to the state legislature. He also engaged in oyster planting and retained his interest in the oyster beds. Courtesy of the Monmouth College Library

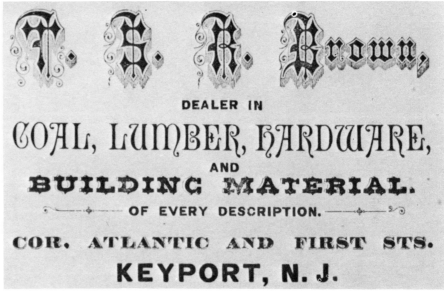

T. S. R. Brown,
DEALER IN
COAL, LUMBER, HARDWARE,
AND
BUILDING MATERIAL.
— OF EVERY DESCRIPTION. —
COR. ATLANTIC AND FIRST STS.
KEYPORT, N. J.

Shown in this 1879 illustration are the mill operated by the Rogers Company on the corner of Main and Monroe avenues in Asbury Park, and the Sullivan Company carpentry shop on the corner of Main and Sewell avenues. Photo from *Historical and Biographical Atlas of the New Jersey Coast, 1879*

One of the main business establishments in Manasquan in the 1870s was Wainwright and Errickson's Dry Goods and Groceries Company. Photo from the *Historical and Biographical Atlas of the New Jersey Coast, 1879*

The original "big store" enterprise was founded as Wardell and Morford in 1835. Morford ran this store pictured at 554 Broadway, Long Branch (near the corner of Norwood Avenue) with his son-in-law A. T. Vanderveer. By 1874 they had to move to larger quarters at 510-512 Broadway. Morford and Vanderveer were purveyors of everything for the home and farm. Courtesy of the Monmouth College Library

72

The New York Store opened on Broadway, Long Branch, on a cash basis in 1867. This modern mart sold dry goods and groceries purchased in New York, Philadelphia, and Newark. The "country people" found a ready market for their produce. Near the close of the century James Tilly Jones conducted a private school for boys on the second floor. Courtesy of the Monmouth College Library

This elegant villa in the Elberon section of Long Branch was completed in 1868. The structure, open to the air and sea vistas, was constructed with a center hall to give the sea breezes access to all the rooms. The house was designed by E. T. Potter, a New York architect, and erected by Jesse C. Stillwell of Long Branch for James M. Brown, a New York banker. The villa is today the Stella Maris Convent, run by the Sisters of Saint Joseph of Peace, Englewood Cliffs, New Jersey. They use the building as a summer retreat and sponsor weekend meetings for engaged couples and youth groups during the off-season. Courtesy of the Monmouth College Library

President Ulysses S. Grant first visited Long Branch in 1869. He took little part in the social life of the resort. At first he stopped at two of the most fashionable hotels, the Mansion House and the Stetson, but their formality and ceremony bored him. Photo courtesy of the Monmouth College Library

73

This cottage was presented to President Grant by a group of Elberon residents, among them George W. Childs; George Pullman; and Moses Taylor, the New York financier. Grant moved into the cottage late in the summer of 1869, and for a dozen years the house at 991 Ocean Avenue, Long Branch was inaccurately referred to as the "Summer Capital." The house was demolished in 1963. Photo courtesy of the Monmouth College Library

President Ulysses S. Grant relaxes at his summer home in Elberon on a summer day in 1872. With him are Mrs. Grant and their youngest son, Jesse. Julia Dent Grant particularly enjoyed the roomy, unpretentious cottage facing the sea. President Grant rose each morning at seven and invariably drove along in his buckboard for twenty miles along the oceanfront. He liked the excitement of a fast drive behind his favorite team of horses. Photo courtesy of the Moss Archives

74

Monmouth County had many black residents throughout its history. This gravestone in Colts Neck is that of Johnson Williams who served during the Civil War. Born in the county and described as a farmer, he was the son of Lucy Williams of Red Bank. Williams was mustered out in Brownsville, Texas in October 1865. Courtesy of the *Register*

This steel engraving appeared in *Picturesque America: Or, the Land We Live In* which was edited by William Cullen Bryant and published in 1872. The subject "'Beacon Hill' crowned by a double-towered light house" was executed by Granville Perkins, a member of the Water Color Society and exhibitor at the National Academy of Design. Perkins, whose specialty was scene painting and illustrating, was a visitor to and portrayer of Long Branch. Courtesy of the Monmouth College Library

This gay scene depicts the opening of the original Monmouth Park Race Track on July 30, 1870. Its grandstand, capable of seating 6,000, was the largest of any racecourse in the United States at that time. The northern half of the grandstand was devoted to ladies accompanied by gentlemen. After twenty years of use, the stand and track shown here were replaced by a new grandstand and track in 1890. Today the 128-acre site on which the track, grandstand, clubhouse, and stables were located is the site of Fort Monmouth. Courtesy of the Monmouth College Library

1884

This coach left the Hollywood Hotel daily for the races at Monmouth Park. Anticipating a successful afternoon at the races are: (from *left* to *right*) Lewis Thompson of Brookdale; Abe Hummel, attorney for Lily Langtry, "Diamond Jim" Brady, and Lillian Russell; John Hoey, president of Adams Express; Andrew Freedman, of B. Altman and Company; Fred Hoey, international pigeon shot; Joseph Morro of Havana; and John S. Hoey, actor. The remaining four passengers are unidentified. Courtesy of the Monmouth College Library

Two horseracing fans are shown on their way to Monmouth Park in 1875. The gentleman on the left in the fancy rig is evidently a member of the upper class. On the right is a caricature of an Irishman in his donkey cart. Perhaps the idea was to show that the racetrack was a democratic place, attracting all classes. Photo courtesy of the Monmouth College Library

76

Heckmann's Confectionary Store was located at the corner of West Main and Throckmorton streets in Freehold. Mr. Heckmann is pictured seated in the wagon in 1875. Photo courtesy of the Freehold Borough Library

Members of the Good Will Fire Company of Freehold pose in front of their firehouse about 1874. Their faithful fire dog is in the center of the photograph. This was the first fire company in Freehold, organized under a charter passed by the legislature in 1872. This building still stands on Throckmorton Street, but is no longer used as a firehouse. Photo courtesy of the Freehold Borough Library

The Princeton Lumber and Improvement Company operated a branch in Asbury Park in the 1870s and 1880s; the main mill and factory were in Princeton, New Jersey. During the winter the company supplied coal to local home owners. Photo from the *Historical and Biographical Atlas of the New Jersey Coast,* 1879

77

G. C. Ormerod operated a boat-building establishment on Main Street in Asbury Park during the latter part of the nineteenth century. He supplied many of the pleasure craft used on the local lakes and rivers. Photo from the *Historical and Biographical Atlas of the New Jersey Coast,* 1879

An illustrator and artist-correspondent for *Harper's Weekly* between 1861 and 1884, Theodore Russell Davis was best known for his illustrations of the Far West. A few years after he drew this scene, Davis, a frequent visitor to the shore, retired and spent the last ten years of his life in Asbury Park. Although spinning rods have taken the place of the old lead squid and handline, the thrill is still the same when the blues hit the surf! Illustration from *Harper's Weekly,* July 3, 1880

78

In 1878 Mr. T. W. Lillagore erected and put into operation a bathing beach and pavilion at Ocean Grove. He made great efforts to see to the safety of his bathers. One could also rent large yachts for sea excursions as well as small rowboats for fishing and rowing on the nearby lake. Photo from the *Historical and Biographical Atlas of the New Jersey Coast,* 1879

This scene is in front of the Ocean Hotel, Long Branch. To the right is a mineral spring pavilion. In order to compete with the mineral springs at Saratoga, Woolman Stokes, the proprietor of the Ocean Hotel, built small pavilions on the beachfront where mineral water was dispensed. The mineral water was probably obtained from a mineral spring located on Monmouth Road in Oakhurst. Illustration from *Harper's Bazaar,* August 17, 1872

79

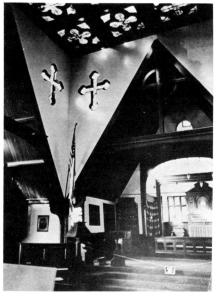

The Ocean Pier at Long Branch was built in 1879; it was 600 feet long and was made of tubular iron, except at the ocean end, where wood was used. It was ten pilings wide. Underneath were 600 bathing cabins, and the promenade deck above, covered with gay-colored awnings, was illuminated by large gas fixtures on tall ornamental posts. Illustration from *Harper's Weekly,* 1883

The Church of the Presidents, on Ocean Avenue in the Elberon section of Long Branch, was built in 1879; when founded it was Saint James Episcopal Church. When the church was established Long Branch was a nationally renowned summer resort populated by the rich and famous; notable worshippers included Presidents Grant, Garfield, Arthur, Wilson, McKinley, and Hayes. The church is now a museum operated by the Long Branch Historical Society. Photo courtesy of the *Register*

In September 1881 President Garfield spent the final agonizing days of his life at Long Branch as he fought to recover from an assassin's bullet. The president came to Elberon from Washington and a special railroad spur was constructed that permitted his railroad car to be brought directly to the front door of the Francklyn cottage. The cottage was offered to the president by Charles Francklyn of the Cunard Line. Garfield died there on September 19, 1881. The cottage was damaged by a fire in 1914, and demolished a few years later. Photo courtesy of the Monmouth College Library

80

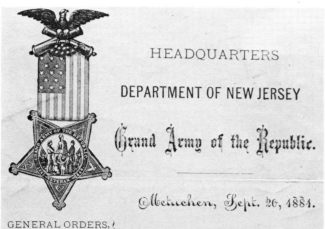

HEADQUARTERS

DEPARTMENT OF NEW JERSEY

Grand Army of the Republic.

Metuchen, Sept. 26, 1881.

GENERAL ORDERS,
NO. 11.

It becomes my painful duty to officially announce the death of the President of the United States, General JAMES A. GARFIELD, which sad event occurred on the 19th inst., at Elberon, Long Branch, within this Department.

The cause of his great suffering and untimely death is too well known.

On the 2d day of July, the telegraph flashed the startling intelligence throughout this broad land and the civilized world, of the dastardly attempt to take his valuable life by assassination. This cowardly and foul act has never but once found its parallel in this free country.

On the 3d day of July the following telegram was sent from these Headquarters:

HEADQUARTERS DEPARTMENT OF NEW JERSEY,
GRAND ARMY OF THE REPUBLIC,
Hon. JAMES G. BLAINE,   Metuchen, July 3, 1881.
Secretary of State, Washington, D. C.,
The Grand Army of the Republic, of this Department, express deep sorrow that the life of their Comrade in War, the Nation's President, has been sought. Please convey to him our loyal and affectionate sympathy. May our Great Commander above preserve his life for the Nation's sake, and if a miracle is needed, Oh! God grant it.
Signed, CHAS. H. HOUGHTON,
R. LLOYD ROBERTS,   Department Commander.
Assistant Adjutant General.

An acknowledgement was promptly received, expressing the thanks of the Cabinet to this Department.

Since that day of terrible suspense, our people have passed through weeks

The day following President Garfield's death at Elberon the Grand Army of the Republic, Department of New Jersey, issued an announcement concerning the passing of their comrade-in-arms. Photo courtesy of the Moss Archives

On September 2, 1918, 25,000 people gathered in Long Branch for the unveiling of a bronze statue of the martyred president, James Abraham Garfield. A lifelong friend of the Garfield family, former United States Senator Theodore E. Burton, represented Ohio at the ceremony and delivered the principal address. Photo from the collection of R. Van Benthuysen

Winslow Homer, one of America's great artists, found the newly fashionable Long Branch a source of inspiration. This century-old wood engraving was the first of five studies Homer was to make of this popular resort. As bathers in the background splash in the sea, three pretty girls pause for a moment. While artist Homer was obviously impressed with *The Beach at Long Branch,* can it be that this young lady was impressed too, as she pensively traced familiar initials in the sand? Illustrations from *Appleton's Journal of Literature and Art,* August 21, 1869

81

The first Hollywood Hotel, shown here, stood on Cedar Avenue in Long Branch. Constructed in 1882 by John Hoey, it was named for the holly trees on the hotel's grounds. After it was destroyed by fire a new Hollywood Hotel was constructed in 1926; this new structure met the same fate in the early 1960s. Photo courtesy of the Monmouth College Library

The American Hotel opened in Freehold around 1837 and was for a time called Monmouth Hall. In the late 1800s it was sold and the new owner Joseph G. Stillwell tore away the old building and erected a good-sized hotel. This advertisement for the hotel, with new owner and an addition, appeared in the 1882 program of the Monmouth County Fair. Today the public rooms display a fine collection of horse pictures and documents of the American Revolution. Courtesy of the Monmouth College Library

AMERICAN HOTEL,
FREEHOLD, N. J.

Having built a large addition to our hotel, we can now furnish all our guests with large and well-ventilated rooms as well as first-class board. We have ample stabling and good box-stalls, also good livery stable attached. For further particulars call on or address

WILLIAM DAVIS,
Proprietor.

James S. Yard, publisher of the (Freehold) *Monmouth Democrat* founded the *Long Branch News* in 1866. He served as editor and publisher. In its lifetime the *News* was a weekly, tri-weekly, and daily. In 1910 the *News* united with the *Long Branch Press* and published under the *Long Branch News and Long Branch Press* banner until 1918. Courtesy of the Monmouth College Library

82

Before 1875 classes were held in this grand old Victorian home at 84 Front Street called the Red Bank Seminary, or Classical Institute. The house was once occupied by composer and bandmaster John Philip Sousa and his family at the turn of the century. In January 1937 the family of Sigmund and Bertha Eisner, the building's last residents, deeded the house to the borough of Red Bank to be used as the new facilities of the Red Bank Public Library. In 1960 the tower was removed, and a two-story addition overlooking the Navesink River was financed by borough and federal grants in 1966. Courtesy of the Monmouth College Library

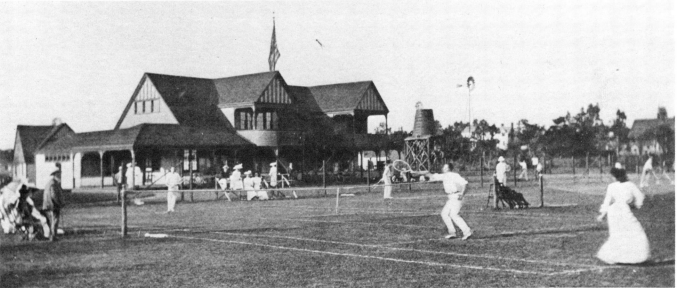

In 1877 the residents of Sea Bright became interested in the game of tennis and organized the Sea Bright Tennis Club in Rumson in 1878. Cricket, baseball, and bowling were added later. The clubhouse, still in use, contains a ballroom and can be converted for theatrical productions. The Sea Bright Lawn and Cricket Club (as it was later renamed), has scheduled tournaments and matches every summer since 1881. The original turf was imported from England. Courtesy of the Monmouth College Library

Joseph F. Chamberlain, "sportsman," built his clubhouse in 1868 on Brighton and Ocean avenues in Long Branch, close to the hotels and cottages. The building cost $40,000, and was designed by Joseph B. Terhune of New York. Parisian in air, the second story piazza was supported by Corinthian-type columns. The mansard roof was covered with multicolored slate, topped by a deck with iron railings. Phil Daly bought the gambling club in 1879. The building became the Wellington Inn in 1907, and was demolished in 1909. Courtesy of the Monmouth College Library

Phil Daly had interests in gambling clubs in Norfolk, Virginia; Philadelphia, and New York. His partner in Chamberlain's old club (renamed the Pennsylvania Club, by the time of this photo), was John Scannel, a Tammany politician. Eight million dollars changed hands each season; the high rollers included the names of Rothschild, Belmont, Gould, and Lorrilard. The double dome was added by Chamberlain in 1876. Courtesy of the Monmouth College Library

84

Scenery painter, book illustrator, and member of the Water Color Society, Granville Perkins produced a number of illustrations of the Jersey Shore. Here, on a cold, blustery morning at Sea Bright, January 7, 1877, he recorded the dramatic breeches buoy rescue of a passenger from the grounded transatlantic steamship *L'Amerique.* As the United States Life Saving Service swung into action, rescuers and rescued huddled by a warming fire. Included in the 216 passengers and crew that were saved was a group of French nuns en route to the Midwest. Illustration from *Harper's Weekly,* January 27, 1877

85

This illustration shows the Lake View House in Asbury Park as it appeared in 1878; at that time the proprietor was A. R. Toland. The hotel was located on the Main Shore Road a short walk from the Asbury Park railroad station. Photo from *Historical and Biographical Atlas of the New Jersey Coast*, 1879

Messrs. Sill and Ripley were the proprietors of the Grand Avenue Hotel in Asbury Park; the building is shown as it appeared in 1878. Photo from the *Historical and Biographical Atlas of the New Jersey Coast*, 1879

This toll bridge was built in 1881 for $30,000. It replaced the Jumping Point wooden drawbridge financed by some of the summer residents and built in 1870. The present concrete double bascule bridge was finished in 1950. Courtesy of the Moss Archives

86

The Coleman House at Asbury Park could comfortably accommodate 500 guests; the owner and proprietor was S. L. Coleman. *The Historical and Biographical Atlas of the New Jersey Coast,* 1879, had this to say about this hotel: "A reading room and finely apportioned billiard hall is provided, where Gentlemen can find in-door 'pastime' and recreation, which together with 'hops' and musical concerts, give to all entertainment of select and charming character." Photo from the *Historical and Biographical Atlas of the New Jersey Coast,* 1879

87

The house owned by Solomon R. Guggenheim on Ocean Avenue in Elberon typified the ornate architecture found on the north Jersey shore in the latter part of the nineteenth century. The residences were festooned with fretwork from porch steps to gable peaks. Because of the numerous architectural features it encompassed, this house was called "Aladdin's Palace." The home was constructed in 1881 by Cornelius Garrison, a railroad and steamship tycoon. Guggenheim purchased the house in 1899; it was demolished in the early 1940s. Photo courtesy of the Monmouth College Library

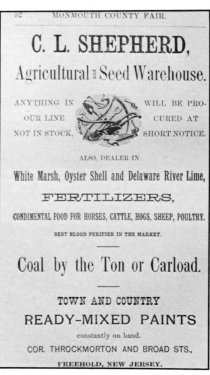

Today as yesterday the farmer could benefit by one-stop shopping. This advertisement in the Monmouth County Fair bulletin of 1882 promised that anything not in stock could be obtained shortly. Courtesy of the Monmouth College Library

When the Hazard Ketchup Factory was in full operation it made Shrewsbury the ketchup capital of the world. The factory opened in 1883 and remained in business until the early 1930s. Photo courtesy of the Moss Archives

The *Jesse Hoyt* ran between New York and Port Monmouth and is pictured here at her Liberty Street (New York) slip. Built at Keyport in 1861, she was 225 feet long with a 32-foot beam. The *Jesse Hoyt* was first purchased by the Raritan and Delaware Bay Railroad Company, then by the Southern Division of the Central Railroad of New Jersey in 1870. Courtesy of the Monmouth College Library

The *Sea Bird*, a paddle wheel steamer, operated between New York and Red Bank during the period 1862 to 1890; this photograph shows her in 1885. Photo courtesy of the Red Bank Public Library

Whether enjoying the water, the sand, or just the sea air from the pier, it was great fun in 1889 to watch the docking of a New York steamer at the Ocean Pier in Long Branch. Courtesy of the Moss Archives

89

Fat, jovial, brassy James Fisk, Junior, bought his way into the Ninth Regiment, New York Militia in 1870 and attained the rank of colonel. Fisk was affiliated with other railroad entrepreneurs, Gould, Drew, and Vanderbilt in his ventures; many regarded him as a public enemy. In the summer of 1868 Fisk and Gould began leasing railroads and steamboats, the *Plymouth Rock* and *Jessie Hoyt* among them. Courtesy of the Moss Archives

The New York and Long Branch Steamboat Company steamer *Elberon* left New York at the foot of Jane Street. Built in 1888 she ran until 1920. The *Elberon* made her calls at Branchport, Pleasure Bay, Sea Bright, and Highlands. The side-wheeler is pictured here in the Shrewsbury River opposite the north beach of Sea Bright. On the left is the Normandy Hotel; the Shrewsbury is on the right. The *Elberon* was sold, and finished her days of service at Providence, Rhode Island. Courtesy of the Moss Archives

On Sundays no freight was carried, but day trippers could leave New York at the foot of West Thirteenth Street or the Battery around 8:30 in the morning and arrive in Long Branch at 11:30. There were trolley connections at West End for Pleasure Bay, and "boat cars" left Asbury Park fifty-five minutes before steamer time at Pleasure Bay. The last steamboat arrived in New York at 7:30 in the evening. Courtesy of the Moss Archives

90

The officers of the National Guard of New Jersey request your presence at a Ball to be given to His Excellency Governor Robert S. Green, at the Beach House, Sea Girt, N.J. on Friday evening, August 26th 1887.

Full dress.

RECEPTION AT
HALF PAST EIGHT O'CLOCK.

In order to build a permanent camp for the National Guard, in 1887 the state government purchased a tract of land in Sea Girt from Commodore Robert F. Stockton, grandson of the signer of the Declaration of Independence. On this land, on a bluff overlooking the ocean, the commodore had built the Beach House, which was later converted into Stockton Hall. After 1906 many governors made the "Little White House" at the National Guard camp their home for three or four months of the year. Courtesy of the Moss Archives

Freehold Ladies Seminary, established in 1845, was accessible to New York and Philadelphia by railroad, steamboat, and plank road. The best teachers were engaged and the most modern techniques were employed to instruct and cultivate the minds and bodies of the young ladies attending. Good habits and ladylike conduct were reinforced by constant references to the Bible; a complete moral, physical, and intellectual education was guaranteed. The playground was "entirely excluded from public observations" and was used for outdoor amusements, tennis, croquet, and calisthenics. Courtesy of the Monmouth County Historical Association

91

In an effort to regain his health Robert Louis Stevenson came to America in 1888, and in the late spring of that year he spent four weeks in Manasquan at the Union House Hotel. He was then at the height of his fame as a leader of the romantic novelists. Will Low, the painter Stevenson had met in France, knew Manasquan well, and it was he who arranged for the writer to stay at the Union House, accompanied by his mother and stepson. On damp days, of which there were many, Stevenson spent much time in his room working on the novel *The Master of Ballantrae*. He usually wrote in bed protected from drafts by a Mexican blanket with a hole in the center through which he slipped his head. Photo courtesy of the Monmouth College Library

A young fisherman accompanies his proud grandfather on a fishing trip. The rest of the fishing fleet bobs up and down, while in the distance commercial party boats steam down from New York to try their luck on the Fishing Banks off Sea Bright. Illustration from *Frank Leslie's Illustrated Newspaper,* July 9, 1887

92

This happy trio is pictured frolicking in the surf at Asbury Park on a hot August day in the 1890s; the bathing apparel they are wearing is typical of the period. Illustration from *Harper's New Monthly Magazine*, August, 1894

Another view of the bathing attire popular in the 1880s and 1890s at Monmouth County seashore resorts. Illustration from *Harper's New Monthly Magazine,* September, 1886

This placid scene of fishermen landing their catch in the surf at Sea Bright in the 1890s belies the rugged existence these men led. To earn their livelihoods from the sea it was necessary to fish in all types of weather and water conditions; the work was hard and the conditions were harsh. Photo courtesy of the Moss Archives

Fishing has been an important Monmouth County industry. Early commercial fishermen used small skiffs of local type to "hand line" offshore. Pound netting, first used within Sandy Hook, was an extremely productive method until the 1950s. This scene at Monmouth Beach shows a heavily loaded "pound boat" landing through the surf. The boat was then hauled up on the beach for unloading using a team harnessed to a sulky. Planks and rollers aided in moving the boat across the sand. In later years tractors or logging hoists were employed. Courtesy of the Moss Archives

The strong bold strokes of marine artist M. J. Burns produced an exciting picture of Sea Bright's fishing fleet landing in a heavy surf. Two hundred and fifty Sea Bright dories, launched in the morning surf, often returned with more than 37,000 pounds of fish for the day's catch. Sometimes, as this picture illustrates, an angry sea forced an empty-handed return. The Octagon Hotel and Peninsula House are depicted at the extreme left of the wood engraving. Illustration from *Harper's Weekly,* November 7, 1891

Before the coming of the white man the Indians gathered native oysters. By the 1840s the supply was depleted and the young, or seed, oysters from the bays to the north and the Chesapeake were used to replenish local beds. Keyport was the center of the oyster trade but towns along the shore of the Navesink and Shrewsbury rivers were also engaged in oystering. Long-handled tongs were used to bring the oysters aboard the skiffs, which were lined with smooth white pine to make shoveling the oysters easier. From the dredge boats they were loaded in baskets and transferred to scows to be brought ashore. In 1892 an oysterman could earn between two dollars and three dollars a day. Courtesy of the Monmouth College Library

95

Arthur A. Zimmerman, the champion bicycle racer of the world in 1892, was born in Camden in 1869. He spent most of his childhood in Manasquan. A member of the Asbury Park Wheelman Club, Zimmerman won his first important victory in 1889. He then went on to capture trophies in England, Germany, France, and Ireland. Later, in Freehold, Zimmerman founded the Burtis and Zimmerman Manufacturing Company which made the Zimmy bicycle. Courtesy of the Monmouth College Library

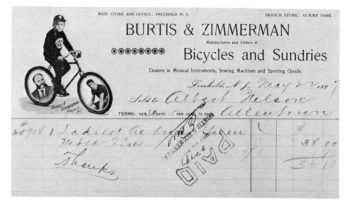

This happy group of bicyclists posed before starting out for a Sunday ride in the 1890s; they are assembled in Allenhurst, a popular resort at the turn of the century. Photograph by Alfred S. Campbell; courtesy of the Red Bank Public Library

96

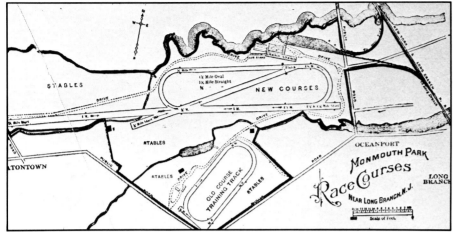

In 1890 an entirely new track was constructed at Monmouth Park. It was immense in its proportions for a track of that day; this is a layout of the new track. Photo courtesy of the Monmouth College Library

The Monmouth County Open Air Horse Show originated in 1893 and was held in Long Branch each year at the end of July. There were sometimes several hundred entrants. For the gentleman there was the excitement and the wagering; the ladies gowned in their best were perhaps more interested in the other ladies, the balls, teas, and other attendant social functions. Courtesy of the Monmouth College Library

97

In 1895 the Fort at Sandy Hook was renamed for Major General Winfield Scott Hancock. With the new name came the added responsibility of coastal defense. These batteries were typical of the fortifications constructed in the period between the 1890s and World War I. Each was mounted with seven-inch siege howitzers, five- and eight-inch siege rifles, and other weapons. Each battery contained eight trained men who were responsible for the maintenance of the equipment. Men who were trained in these gun placements were sent to France in 1918. Courtesy of the Gateway National Recreation Area, Sandy Hook Unit

This view shows Main Street in Freehold in 1895. Photo courtesy of the Monmouth County Historical Association

Simon Lake, an American inventor, designed his submarine to be used primarily for locating sunken ships, removing cargoes, raising ships, and floating those stranded on sandbars. It could also be used to remove obstructions from harbors and rivers. The submarine was designed to carry six men, reach a depth of 300 feet, and work on the bottom for forty-eight hours. It was tested in the Shrewsbury River. In 1898 the *Argonaut* and her crew travelled 2,000 miles, working along the Atlantic Coast. Prior to World War I, the Russians adapted Lake's design and the Austro-Hungarian submarines were Lake prototypes. The town of Atlantic Highlands has a wooden replica on display. Courtesy of the Monmouth College Library

98

Two hard-handed and strong-backed Atlantic Highlands watermen rowed across the Atlantic in 1896. The voyage from New York to LeHavre took sixty-two days in the *Fox,* a modified Sea Bright skiff constructed by William Seaman of Branchport. The after end of the hull was projected to a canoe stern instead of the traditional transom stern. Harold L. Seaman, then a youngster, aided his elders by "bucking" the copper rivet fastenings, being small enough to crawl into the recesses in the hull. The members of the Long Branch Ice Boat and Yacht Club decided to construct a facsimile of the original, the lines of which were reconstructed by Harold L. "Pappy" Seaman from memory and old records at the age of 92. In 1975 the club membership turned to and produced *Fox II* under the supervision of "Pappy." The new *Fox* was rowed to the Mystic Seaport Museum for temporary exhibition and returned to its permanent Monmouth County home. Photo courtesy of the *Register*

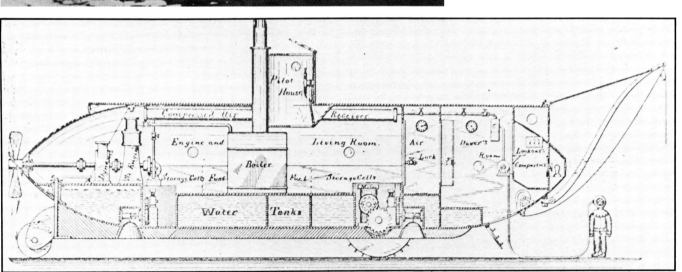

In the 1890s and early 1900s railroad companies published brochures which promoted towns at the seashores and mountains along their routes. These booklets contained descriptive and statistical information; train schedules; and directories of hotels, cottages, and boardinghouses. This Pennsylvania Railroad Company bulletin of 1892 concentrated on the shore area. Courtesy of the Monmouth College Library

Stephen Crane, the author of *The Red Badge of Courage,* was born in Newark, New Jersey, but at an early age his family moved to Asbury Park. His brother Townley, who was twenty years his senior, conducted a news service for the *New York Herald Tribune* and other metropolitan newspapers. When he was seventeen years of age Stephen went to work for his brother gathering news of the summer resorts and writing stories of clambakes and sailing parties. In the summer of 1892 a controversial story he wrote for the *Tribune* concerning a political parade in Asbury Park cost both Stephen and Townley their jobs with the newspaper. Photo courtesy of the Monmouth College Library

With arrangements made for baggage, the steamboat with its train connection was certainly the most pleasant way to travel to the shore. The steamboat companies offered the passengers good food and music in comfort, fresh air, and splendid scenery. Posters such as this one also lured city dwellers to the seashore for the day. Courtesy of the Moss Archives

100

Vredenburgh Rifles, COMPANY E, 7TH REG., N. G. S. N. J., FREEHOLD, N. J.

Annual Reception and Drill.

72 Freehold Opera House, February 21, 1895.

TICKETS $1.50.

Admit Mr. and Lady

Not Transferable.

Clubs, lodges, societies, as well as churches were an integral part of the social life of Freehold. After the Civil War returning military groups remained close. This ticket admits two to the annual reception of the Vredenburgh Rifles. The company was named for local hero, Major Peter Vredenburgh, Junior, who was killed in the battle of Winchester, Virginia in 1864. Courtesy of the Moss Archives

In 1865 the Astor House Hotel Company purchased the Conover House on the south end of the bluff in Long Branch for $60,000. Incorporating the old hotel, the company erected this imposing structure of 300 rooms. Its construction was unique for the shore area—L-shaped and lacking the sweeping porches or galleries so common to the resorts. This design ensured greater privacy and safety from prowlers and thieves. The value of the property, hotel building, and other refinements approached $400,000. Managed by Charles A. Stetson, Junior, the hotel was first class, and charged its guests accordingly. Courtesy of the Monmouth College Library

Standing in front of the Atlantic Highlands Post Office in the late 1890s are: Murray Foster, Sam Brown, George Conover, Sam Bartheson, Stephen Powell, Frank Price, Howard Manning, and William M. Foster. Photo courtesy of the Monmouth County Historical Association

101

S. D. Moss and his coachman Charlie Jones are taking the sea air. This tintype was taken in 1899 opposite the Cranmer Baths on Ocean Avenue, Long Branch. Courtesy of the Moss Archives

In this 1890s photograph, a horse-drawn wagon from the Van Brunt and Sons Stables in Matawan is about to start off for a day's work. The firm was formerly the Matawan Stage Line. Photo courtesy of the Monmouth County Historical Association

102

Buffalo Bill's Wild West Show is shown at the campgrounds on Morris Avenue in Long Branch in the year 1899. Photograph from the Durnell Collection, Monmouth College Library

Dan Rice (1823-1900) is remembered as one of the greatest of American clowns; he was also famous as a cracker-box philosopher and commentator on public affairs. Rice made his last circus tour in 1885. He then returned to West Long Branch where he lived with relatives.

During his lifetime he made several fortunes. His generosity to friends, poor investments, and business reverses left Dan practically penniless in the last days of his life. When he died there was no money to pay for his funeral and a marker was not placed on his grave. Louis Barbour, a Rice descendant, was instrumental in arranging a Dan Rice Day which was observed on October 17, 1976. Donations from this occasion were used to purchase a marker. Photo courtesy of the West Long Branch Historical Society

At the height of his popularity in the 1850s and 1860s Dan Rice commanded a salary of $1,000 a week. Circus owners fought for his services. When he died in West Long Branch, aged seventy-seven, the *New York Times* obituary gave the once great clown only two paragraphs. Photo courtesy the West Long Branch Historical Society

Garret Augustus Hobart, the twenty-fourth vice president of the United States, was born in West Long Branch. Hobart was the son of Addison Willard and Sophia (Vanderveer) Hobart. His father was a teacher at the Long Branch Academy. He graduated from Rutgers College in 1863, studied law, and was admitted to the New Jersey bar in 1866. He accepted the nomination for vice president in 1896, on the ticket with William McKinley, and was elected. Hobart never severed his ties with Monmouth County. In the late 1890s he summered at Monmouth Beach, and in 1899 he rented Normanhurst, a palatial mansion that stood on the site of the present-day Guggenheim Memorial Library in West Long Branch. Photo courtesy of the West Long Branch Historical Society

The Parker Farm, 275 acres on Rockwell Avenue, Long Branch was sliced up at a sheriff's sale. A piece of the land passed through a succession of owners until purchased by Dr. Jacob H. and Cornelius Vanderveer in the 1860s. Dr. Vanderveer was the veterinary surgeon for the Long Branch area. He and Cornelius built their farmhouse on seventy acres of worked farmland, painted it a pale yellow, and trimmed the columns and cornices a dark brown. Behind the house lay the barns and hospital stables. The house was razed in the 1920s. Courtesy of the Monmouth College Library

Branchport (now part of Long Branch) was a center in its own right during the last century. It was the terminus of a boat line connecting with New York. Branchport had restaurants, an amusement area, and hotels. The Hotel Norwood, shown here, was modified and still exists as Bobby Byrne's River Edge Restaurant. Courtesy of the Monmouth College Library

Spanish-American War soldiers from
the Freehold area had this picture taken
at Pompton Lakes Camp in 1899. Photo
courtesy of the Freehold Borough
Library

A group of off-duty Spanish-American War troopers from the Red Bank area pose with their rifles and swords. Photo courtesy of the Red Bank Public Library

Teddy Roosevelt's former regiment of Rough Riders, originally 11,000 strong, was down to 200 in 1900. In brown sombreros and jingling spurs the Riders drilled and entertained summer residents up and down the shore. Courtesy of the Monmouth College Library

While Great Wars Rage: 1900~1945

Monmouth County was on the edge of change in 1900, but agriculture remained the predominant occupation. Life across the predominantly rural countryside was still relatively simple. It was a splendid time. Most residents of the county felt that way as they welcomed the twentieth century. There was ample reason for high hopes and general satisfaction.

Monmouth County housewives found stores well stocked and prices low: they could buy eggs for twelve cents a dozen, sirloin steak for twenty-four cents a pound, and a turkey dinner for twenty cents.

At the turn of the century the founding fathers of Monmouth County shore resorts had a variety of goals. Some wanted fashionable exclusiveness for their towns; some wanted religious exclusiveness; others wanted vacation spots for teetotalers; and some saw dollar signs in demon rum. Some wanted quiet while others wanted noise.

As Monmouth County entered the twentieth century, it simultaneously embraced the automobile.

Almost everyone was fascinated by the frail, costly, balky contraptions that, as one owner described them, "shook and trembled and clattered, spat oil, fire and smoke." By 1904, according to a display advertisement in the *Asbury Park Press,* shore residents could buy a Ford with two cylinders, "no vibration, and a speed of eight to thirty miles an hour." The first garage in Asbury Park was established by C. R. Zacharias, whose first customer brought in a Locomobile to have it repaired.

In 1908 Long Branch introduced automobile races to the shore area; the races were held at Elkwood Park. This may have, in some small measure, compensated for the lack of gambling. The New Jersey state legislature had recently outlawed gambling in casinos and wagering on horse races. The people could now watch cars tear along at fifty or sixty miles an hour. The greatest attraction that season was a well advertised and attended match between four of the fastest automobiles of the country, one of which was Barney Oldfield's "Green Dragon." Two of the other cars were foreign-made (a Mercedes and a Renault), while the fourth car was an American Packard.

Many readers will remember the gas lines of the late 1970s. In the early 1900s the problem of procuring gasoline in Monmouth County was also a pressing one. There were no gasoline pumps as we know them. Gasoline was poured from a five-gallon can most likely purchased at the general store. On holiday weekends the problem of securing gasoline became particularly acute at shore resorts.

Unquestionably the most important event in Monmouth County's pre-World War I history was its revival as the summer capital. President Woodrow Wilson felt keenly the necessity of returning to his adopted state to wage his campaign for re-election. Therefore, when Captain J. B. Greenhut offered

Shadow Lawn, his palatial estate at West Long Branch, as a summer capital, it was promptly accepted. Wilson was careful to say that he would not accept the mansion without paying a rental fee; he donated $2,500 to local charities.

Shadow Lawn was already an architectural and financial legend when President Wilson lifted it to national attention. It had been the dream house of John A. McCall, president of the New York Life Insurance Company. In July 1903 the *Long Branch Record* reported that McCall had decided to erect a "handsome country seat" on sixty-five acres of land he had assembled. The mansion was completed in 1905. Unfortunately, McCall died the following year and the estate was sold to Captain Greenhut in 1909.

Workers are shown preparing tomatoes for canning in a factory at Red Bank at about the turn of the century. The factory was located where the Marine Park tennis courts now stand. Photo courtesy of the Red Bank Public Library

110

It was at Shadow Lawn on September 2, 1916 that Wilson received the official notification of the Democratic Party that he would be their standard bearer for the presidency. Most of the leading Democratic statesmen and politicians of the day assembled at Shadow Lawn, where Senator Ollie James of Kentucky delivered the principal speech.

After the official notification, Wilson conducted his fight for re-election from Shadow Lawn. It was the old-fashioned type of front porch campaign in which the public came to the candidate. Actually, it was a front lawn campaign, for most of the meetings were held on the vast lawn that faced the south facade of the estate.

Wilson was at Shadow Lawn to receive the election results. Early returns were far from encouraging. They showed his Republican opponent, Charles Evans Hughes, the leader by a substantial margin. The results still were not clear the next day, until the returns came in from the western states and the tide changed in Wilson's favor, making him the eventual winner.

The two world conflicts during the first half of the twentieth century brought deep repercussions to the social and economic life of Monmouth County. The influx of military personnel, the construction of new military bases, the close proximity of German submarines offshore, the departure of young men and women for the service, and the work of civilians in defense activities—all had widespread effects on the lives of the county's residents.

The most important development in Monmouth County during World War I was the establishment of Camp Alfred Vail as the Signal Corps Center. On May 16, 1917, about five weeks after America entered the war, construction began on the site of the old Monmouth Park racetrack in Little Silver. Buildings and barracks were erected in May and June, and the camp received its first troops on July 9. It remained Camp Alfred Vail until August 6, 1925, when the post became Fort Monmouth in honor of its proximity to the site of one of the most important battles of the Revolutionary War.

An army of hastily recruited carpenters, plumbers, and electricians constructed the camp, and many a farmer turned "carpenter" in view of the four-dollar-a-day wages. What turned out was more a miracle of haste than a monument to good architecture.

One Monmouth County manufacturer took advantage of the demand for flying machines—Inglis M. Uppercu, who in 1914 began taking orders for allied seaplanes at his Aeromarine Plane and Motor Company in Keyport. Soon Aeromarine covered sixty-six acres, and used sixteen buildings to make hydroplane trainers and a "flying boat" for the navy.

A few years following the Armistice, Monmouth County entered another warlike era. Prohibition came closer to dividing the county into two camps than anything since the Revolutionary War. The county's attitude toward Prohibition agents in the 1920s was very like that of a resistance movement toward an army of occupation. Throughout the long reign of the eighteenth amendment the shore area echoed and re-echoed with scandal, punctured occasionally by a shot aimed at (or by) a bootlegger, or by a Coast Guard vessel at a rum runner. The public thought it needed alcohol; why did the Coast Guard have to interfere with their source of supply?

Rum runners flaunted their power on Raritan and Sandy Hook bays and the Monmouth County

111

beachfront as well as the riverways. The boats of the rum runners were so powerful they outran those of the Coast Guard, particularly during the early years of Prohibition. Pitched battles offshore between the rum runners and the Coast Guard brought sounds of gunfire shoreward on midnight breezes. Prohibition put the Coast Guard in a thankless position. The public thought it needed alcohol. Political aid, public opinion, and money were on the side of the rum runners.

A small armada of Monmouth County fishermen found cases of scotch a far better haul than a load of fish. Bridge tenders along the shore developed the ability to raise bridges for rum-filled boats and lower them in the face of the Coast Guard pursuers.

One bootlegging operation, controlled by a powerful shortwave radio station from atop the Atlantic Highlands, smuggled in 10,000 illegal cases of liquor a week, valued at between $50 and $100 a case. Speakeasy patrons generally received drinks cut by a third, so estimated retail sales of the Atlantic Highlands supply alone totaled more than $100 million.

No doubt the citizens of Monmouth County hailed the repeal of the eighteenth amendment in 1933, but their elation was probably somewhat tempered as they struggled with the difficulties brought on by the depression. Some may have cast their eyes to the western fringes of the county where the federal government was taking positive steps to ease the plight of some idle men. The plan was to decentralize industry and combat unemployment. What evolved was the establishment of Jersey Homesteads.

This was the visionary experiment in communal living sponsored by the Federal Resettlement Administration. Jewish garment workers from New York City and Philadelphia were to be relocated and

Sleighs and buggies were driven along snow-covered Broad Street in Red Bank at the turn of the century. Photo from *Red Bank on the Navesink* by Helen C. Phillips

given the opportunity to get a new lease on life.

What developed was a controversial, nationally publicized program to build a utopian-type community in Manalapan Township. Starting with an undeveloped, 1,270-acre wooded tract, the federal government gave architects and planners the go-ahead to use their imagination to build a community of 200 ranch-type homes on half-acre sites. Upwards of 1,000 Works Projects Administration workers from Monmouth County built the homes.

To support the residents, the government constructed a communal building to be used as a clothing factory, and left more than 400 acres for a community farming project.

The homes pioneered new construction methods like precast walls, prefabrication, baseboard and other types of heating, and solid masonry or cinder block construction.

The peak of Jersey Homesteads came in 1938. The community of 200 homes were built, 120 Jewish families were resettled, and nearly 100 workers were employed in a cooperative clothing factory. But by the end of 1939 the Farm Bureau

Administration declared the cooperative projects to be failures. The clothing factory was sold at auction, and in 1940 the farm cooperative was liquidated.

The government decided Jersey Homesteads should become strictly a "suburban housing project." In 1947 the government sold the homes to individuals. When President Franklin Roosevelt died, the residents unanimously and almost immediately decided to change the municipality to Roosevelt.

The main activities in Monmouth County during World War II were concentrated at the Earle Naval Ammunition Depot and at Fort Monmouth. The site of the $14 million ammunition depot, chosen in 1943, was an 8,400-acre tract of land ten miles southeast of Red Bank. The depot was to provide ammunition storage and shipment facilities for naval units operating in the New York area. The reservation was named for Admiral Ralph Earle,

112

In the winters, at the turn of the century, it was a common thing to find the men in the back room of Phil Stofell's Cigar Store on Broad Street, in Red Bank, playing hearts. The players are, *left to right,* Borden Wolcutt, Pop Bloomberg, Thomas Updyke, Arch Antonides, Arch Harveland, and Will Hockma. Courtesy of the *Register*

Chief of the Navy's Bureau of Ordnance in World War I.

Each month the ammunition depot sent nearly 130,000 tons of munitions eastward to help seal Hitler's doom. At times Earle stored enough explosives to blow New Jersey and New York City off the map, but fortunately, it all went elsewhere.

Many Monmouth County resort hotels were taken over by the government at various times during the war. At Asbury Park, the British Navy leased the Monterey Hotel and the Berkeley-Carteret. In May 1942, a hotel at Shark River was taken over by the War Department as part of expanding Camp Evans, a subpost of Fort Monmouth, for use as a radar laboratory.

Submarine depredations during World War II reached more serious proportions than World War I, and brought intensive activity on the part of the Naval Air Patrol. As destruction by submarines grew worse, it became evident that the ships at sea were silhouetted against beachfront lights; they were easy prey for the U-Boats. In March 1942, the Army ordered a permanent coastal "dimout" in an attempt

to halt the sinking of ships off the Jersey beaches.

Eighteen months after it started, the dimout was supplanted by the "brownout." This was strictly voluntary and designed to conserve electricity. ●

This photo shows the first home of the Elks on Front Street in Red Bank as it appeared in the 1920s. Formerly the residence of Homie Hendrickson, the home was later purchased by the Eisner family and demolished. Photo courtesy of the Red Bank Public Library

113

In this photograph, circa 1900, workers are constructing the roadbed for the new trolley line from Red Bank to Long Branch. The trolley ran every half hour from Broad Street to Monmouth Street, through Shrewsbury to Eatontown on the way to Long Branch. Photo courtesy of the Red Bank Public Library

This is the house constructed for Lydia and Alonzo Sherman on Bath Avenue in Long Branch in 1900. Standing in front of the home, from *left to right*, are Lydia Walton Sherman. Walton Sherman Jr., Adeline Sherman, unknown, George Walton, Sadie Paterson, and Jemima L. Walton. Photo courtesy of Charles H. Maps Junior

114

This turn-of-the-century scene shows a group of volunteer firemen about to start a parade in Red Bank. Photo courtesy of the Red Bank Public Library

In the early 1900s the Ford and Miller Shoe Store of Red Bank used this float in a borough parade. John R. Bergen started the business in 1846. In 1898, the Bergen business was bought by Albert S. Miller and Benjamin Ford, both of whom were clerks employed by the firm. In 1912 Mr. Miller bought Ford's interest and the business became known as Albert S. Miller Shoe Company. It has been operating under the name since that time. Photo courtesy of the Red Bank Public Library

This gaily decorated automobile participated in a parade in Red Bank in the early 1900s. Photo courtesy of the Red Bank Public Library

In the early 1900s the trolley from Red Bank traveled north up Route 35 to Tyndall Road in Middletown, and then to Campbells Junction. Here the line divided—one branch headed for Belford and Perth Amboy; the other turned south to Highlands and the beach. There were several stops along the route as this was the main mode of transportation. Trolley lines networked the state. From this station at Keansburg one could travel to New York, and, given perseverance, to Philadelphia. Courtesy of the Monmouth College Library

This bridge, looking like a giant's toy, was dedicated on May 18, 1901; it was the third and grandest connection between Sea Bright and Rumson. The bridge was typical for its day. On gruelling summer days the metalwork would expand in the blistering sun and have to be hosed down with cold water before it could be closed. This bridge was replaced in 1950. Courtesy of the Monmouth College Library

Guglielmo Marconi, the radio pioneer, established a temporary radio transmitter on the Highlands of the Navesink in 1899. Capable of sending messages as far as New York, the transmitter was used to report the America's Cup races (sailed off Sandy Hook) to New York newspapers in Morse code.

The hilly area on the west side of Shark River, a few miles from Belmar, appeared attractive as the site of a trans-Atlantic transmitter. It was there the Marconi Company established a station and 100-foot high structural steel towers mounted on concrete that were used in the pioneer effort, on December 12, 1901. The property was later acquired by the Signal Corps as the Camp Evans part of Fort Monmouth. Of the network of over thirty towers one remains in good condition. The concrete standards dot neighborhood backyards. Courtesy of the *Register*

Field and heavy artillery guns were mounted for test firing at the proof battery on the north beach of the Sandy Hook Proving Ground. Brooklyn, Staten Island, Manhattan, and New Jersey residents became used to the big booms which rattled china closets and sent cats under beds.

The shifting of sand due to beach erosion has unearthed live mines and ammunition, and Gateway National Recreation Area was forced to close for safety measures during the winter and spring of 1980-1981. Presently more artifacts are coming to light as a result of the beach nourishment program; the finds are being returned to the Sandy Hook Museum for future display. Courtesy of the Gateway National Recreation Area, Sandy Hook Unit

In 1902 this 16-inch coast artillery rifle was the largest gun ever built. It was tested at the Sandy Hook Proving Ground. The projectile weighed 2,400 pounds and had a range of twenty-one miles. Courtesy of the Monmouth College Library

When the West Long Branch Fire Department was formed in 1902 the borough had not yet separated from Eatontown; this separation occurred in 1908. The first apparatus, shown here, was a steel frame truck equipped with chemical tanks and ladders. On side of truck, from *left to right,* are Harry Smith, Bert White, Frank S. Dennis, Frank Sherman. The driver is Freeman Howland, and seated with the driver, holding a trophy, is Samuel Bowman. Photo courtesy of the Monmouth College Library

118

The Young Men's Bible Class of the Baptist Church of Freehold pose in front of their church at the turn of the century. Photo courtesy the Monmouth County Historical Association

Fritz Heinish was a town character in Freehold about 1902. He lived on Court Street, opposite the present courthouse, and made his living selling rat and mouse traps. Photo courtesy of the Freehold Borough Library

Interior view of Karagheusian Rug Company mill in Freehold, which began operation in 1894. In the 1930s Karagheusian employed 2,500 workers who maintained round-the-clock production at the facility. The plant closed in 1965. Photo courtesy of the Monmouth County Historical Association

This aerial view shows the former Karagheusian Rug Company mill. Today it is the largest commercial rental building in Monmouth County. The building's large brick smokestacks, no longer needed but too expensive to remove, still bear the company's name. Photo courtesy of the Monmouth County Historical Association

120

These workers were harvesting hay on the former William Thompson farm in 1903. The Brockway Glass Plant, Highway 33, in Freehold now occupies this site. The men in the picture, from *left to right,* are William N. Thompson, George Blair, Frank Blair, unknown, Bill Blair, and Henry Hance. The boy is unidentified. Photo courtesy of the Freehold Borough Library

In 1903 Andrew Carnegie donated $10,000 to the borough of Freehold to cover the construction costs of a public library. Built on the south side of East Main Street, its cornerstone was put in place on October 19, 1903. Photo courtesy of the Freehold Borough Library

The Freehold chapter of the Knights of Pythias is pictured on an annual outing at Port-Au-Peck in the early 1900s. Photo courtesy of the Freehold Borough Library

121

The original Shadow Lawn mansion in West Long Branch was built in 1903 by John A. McCall, president of the New York Life Insurance Company, on an estate of thirty-five acres. The colonial frame structure, designed by Henry Edward Creiger, contained fifty-two rooms. The building had a lavish front portico, supported by ten massive columns, with a small bandstand at each end. The mansion was destroyed by fire in 1927. Photo courtesy of the Monmouth College Library

This interior view shows the social hall of the original Shadow Lawn mansion constructed in 1903. It was here that Woodrow Wilson entertained guests when he used the home as the summer White House in 1916. Photo courtesy of the Monmouth College Library

122

This is an early photograph of Arthur W. Pryor, trombonist, bandmaster, composer, and recording artist. In 1892, Pryor became the featured trombonist with the newly formed band of John Philip Sousa. In 1903 Pryor formed his own band and for the next seventeen summers performed regularly during the summer season at Asbury Park. He retired in 1933 to a farm at West Long Branch where he taught music at his leisure. He died there and was buried in the local Glenwood Cemetery. Photo courtesy of the Asbury Park Public Library

The Carlisle Indian band paraded and presented concerts along the shore in the early 1900s. Carlisle Institute was established at Carlisle, Pennsylvania in 1879 by the United States Indian Affairs Department. The school offered a five-year degree program for Indians, some of whom, on arrival, could not speak English. The Aborigines, Carlisle's football team, played Harvard and Princeton. Courtesy of the Monmouth College Library

123

This Red Bank couple decorated their electric with flowers and enjoyed an automobile fete circa 1905. Photo courtesy of the Moss Archives

Even in the early 1900s basketball was a popular sport in Freehold. One of the fine teams was Company "G" of the Vredenburgh Rifles. In this 1903 photo, *top row,* are Joe Thompson, John Heiser, William Freeman, and Edward Collins; *bottom row,* Frank Hurley, Harry Bailey, George Quigg, Dr. Harvey S. Brown, and Al Mooney. Photo courtesy of the Freehold Borough Library

Houseboat living is not a new idea. This homemade river summer home is anchored off the Highland Beach bath houses in the Shrewsbury river in the early 1900s. Today sailing craft and yachts anchor for group fun and sport in the quiet coves of the river. Courtesy of the Monmouth College Library

The several iceboat clubs on the Shrewsbury and Navesink Rivers were strong competitors, establishing formalized racing by 1900. Members competed with other distant clubs along the mid-Hudson River, New York lakes, and elsewhere. This scene is close to the old railroad bridge across the Shrewsbury, on the north side. Courtesy of the Monmouth College Library

This tent community on the shores of the Shrewsbury river in Highlands is near the spot where Joshua Huddy was hanged in 1782. These vacation camps were common sightings along the river in the early 1900s. Courtesy of the Monmouth College Library

This photograph of the Elberon railroad station in the early 1900s shows the transition from horse-drawn carriages to automobiles. At the time automobiles were called "rich men's toys" and worse. Photo courtesy of the Newark Public Library

Ann May Hospital on Vroom and First avenues in Spring Lake was the predecessor of the present Jersey Shore Medical Center in Neptune. The hospital was started between 1903 and 1905 as a nursing facility with a homeopathic slant. It grew rapidly to a general hospital which required larger facilities, finally moving to a new modern building in Neptune in 1932. The remaining part of the 1932 building has been dwarfed by the additions since. Courtesy of the Ann May School of Nursing Archives, Jersey Shore Medical Center

This happy group of ocean bathers is shown at the Octagon House beach in Sea Bright in 1904. Skirts, pantalettes, and long stockings were standard bathing attire for women during this period. Photo courtesy of the Moss Archives

Organized in 1692 by Scotch settlers, the First Presbyterian Church was the earliest church in Matawan. In 1767 the church burned and was rebuilt in 1798. Sometime between 1889 and 1893 alterations were made to the front of the church. Stanford White of McKim, Mead & White, architect of many elegant shore homes, designed the steeple and front facade. Heavily insured, indebted, and in sore need of repairs, the church was fired in 1955 by a parishioner who mistakenly thought that the insurance money would rebuild and restore the building. Photo courtesy of Matawan-Aberdeen Public Library

Murry Guggenheim (1858-1939) financier and philanthropist, was the third of eight sons of Meyer Guggenheim, a Swiss immigrant, who, with the aid of his sons built up a vast fortune through holdings in copper, silver, lead, and gold mines. Murry began spending summers in Long Branch in the 1890s and built his mansion in West Long Branch in 1905. Photo courtesy of the Monmouth College Library

The Guggenheim Cottage was constructed in 1905. The building was designed by Carrere and Hastings, architects whose works included the main building of the New York Public Library. The design of the estate earned them the Gold Medal of the New York Chapter of the American Institute of Architects in 1903. Pictured is the south facade of the home showing the reflecting pool. Photo courtesy of the Monmouth College Library

128

This is a view of the Guggenheim Cottage, now the Monmouth College Library, taken shortly after the home was constructed in 1905. The view shows the formal gardens and the entrance to the building beneath the porte cochere. Photo courtesy of the Monmouth College Library

The Guggenheim Foundation of New York City donated the former summer home of Murry and Leonie Guggenheim to Monmouth College in 1960 with the provision that it be converted to use as a library. The building was added to the National Register of Historic Sites in 1978. Photo courtesy of the Monmouth College Library

This photograph of the Freehold Raceway in the early 1900s is yet another view of the transition from horse-drawn carriages to autmobiles. The automobiles were still a novelty. They took a back seat to the horse-drawn vehicles. Like all new gadgets, the car became a necessary symbol that established status. Photo courtesy of the Newark Public Library

129

Steamboats, generally side-wheelers, carried much of the freight in Monmouth County during the early days, and were a pleasant way to travel during the summer. The photograph shows *Albertina* iced in at Red Bank near the present wharf about 1906. Courtesy of the Moss Archives

The surfboat stations of the Life Saving Service dotted the shoreline at short intervals; the beach in between was patrolled at short intervals by the members of the crew. This 1906 photo of the station at Avon shows the crew and their New Jersey-model, square stern, surfboat. The boats were constructed of cedar, usually by local builders. They were later replaced by double-ended surfboats of various models. Courtesy of the Moss Archives

These men are about to enjoy a libation or two at the "liquor tent" at the 1906 Monmouth County Fair, held in Middletown Township. The grounds were adjacent to the firehouse property on Route 35. The imposing gentlemen are (from left to right) Charlie A. Hawkins, under sheriff of Monmouth County; Charles MacDonald, Democratic assemblyman; William O'Brien; David Crater, surrogate; and Charlie Straus. Courtesy of the Moss Archives

130

In the 1800s Keansburg (then Granville) had a church and a few businesses. By the turn of the century people were pitching tents, and the town was overrun with summer visitors. There were not enough boardinghouses. William A. Gelhaus and his development company planned a new Keansburg in 1906. They laid out Beachway, some new streets, a dance hall, and hotel. Soon there were fifteen hotels and throngs of people. Courtesy of the Monmouth College Library

From the latter part of the nineteenth century to the 1940s, fox hunting was a colorful and popular sport in Monmouth County. Now, housing developments have closed the open spaces and for the most part driven the fox away.

In this photograph, taken in 1907, we see a group of fox hunters assembled in Shrewsbury prior to the start of the chase. Photo courtesy of the Shrewsbury Historical Society

131

Fishing and boatbuilding were important industries in Monmouth County. Shore fishing increased during the mid years of the nineteenth century, centered at Sea Bright and Nauvoo (the present Monmouth Beach). By the turn of the century several hundred skiffs fished from these and other beaches. This 1909 picture of a part of a fleet at Sea Bright shows examples of a type of fishing boat which originated and developed in the region, the Sea Bright Skiff. By 1909 many had abandoned propulsion by oar and sail switched to power. A number of the boats in this picture have been converted to gasoline power. Courtesy of Dr. Peter J. Guthorn

No. 41 Fishing Boats   Sea Bright N.J.   Foxwell

Another adaptation of the Sea Bright Skiff was the Pound Boat, designed for launching from the beach and servicing offshore fish traps or "pound nets." Here a crew is emptying the catch from a pound net. This type of fishing was abandoned about 1950. Courtesy of Dr. Peter J. Guthorn

"Seven men catch 375 fish" might be the title of this photograph. The men were from Keyport and the year was about 1910. Photo courtesy of the Monmouth County Historical Association

132

Master George Morris, dressed as a colonial, sits atop his hydrangea-decorated cart. The occasion is the 1910 Long Branch Baby Parade. Courtesy of the Moss Archives

The City Market, a grocery and butcher shop, was owned by the Doremus brothers. Although the packaging has changed, many of the items seen on the shelves are available today. This photo was taken on July 20, 1910 by Coleman, the photographer. Courtesy of the Moss Archives

A familiar sight on Red Bank streets about 1910 was this horse-drawn water sprinkler used to keep dust down. Photo courtesy of the Red Bank Public Library

Charles W. Irwin of Red Bank stands in the doorway of his blacksmith shop in about 1911; his seated friend is unknown. Photo courtesy of the Red Bank Public Library

Members of Steamer Company No. 1 of the Freehold Fire Department gather for an anniversary celebration in 1911 at the rear of No. 1 Court House Square. Established in 1874, this was the second fire company established in Freehold. Photo courtesy of the Freehold Borough Library

It's a Foxwell photo.

The rivers were used extensively for pleasure as well as commerce. With club pennants flying these spectators are enjoying a summer regatta on the Shrewsbury River in 1911. The ladies are protected from the sun by awnings and boat canopies, the gentlemen by their straw boaters and panamas. Courtesy of the Monmouth College Library

The many lakes along the shore towns were pleasant areas to spend a summer day. These sedately propelled, canopied rowboats on Wesley Lake, between Asbury Park and Ocean Grove, provided limited and safe excursions on the water. Courtesy of the Monmouth College Library

Theodore Roosevelt was no stranger to Monmouth County. When he was twelve years old he suffered from asthma and was brought to the salubrious pines in Lower Squankum, Howell Township for a cure. During his presidency Roosevelt appeared in Sea Girt in 1902 and Ocean Grove in 1905. In 1912 he was running for president on the Progressive party platform against Willliam Howard Taft. On May 25, 1912 Roosevelt spoke in Freehold from the courthouse steps, visited the Battle of Monmouth monument, traveled by auto to Farmingdale, and by train to Asbury Park, Long Branch, Red Bank, and Matawan. Roosevelt was well received in these places; his public carried flags and the towns were gaily decorated with bunting. Courtesy of the Monmouth College Library

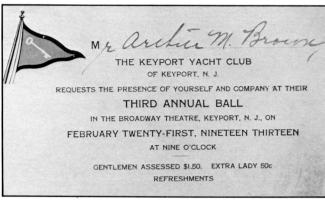

Mr. Arthur M. Brown

THE KEYPORT YACHT CLUB
OF KEYPORT, N. J.

REQUESTS THE PRESENCE OF YOURSELF AND COMPANY AT THEIR

THIRD ANNUAL BALL

IN THE BROADWAY THEATRE, KEYPORT, N.J., ON

FEBRUARY TWENTY-FIRST, NINETEEN THIRTEEN

AT NINE O'CLOCK

GENTLEMEN ASSESSED $1.50.   EXTRA LADY 50c
REFRESHMENTS

The village of Keyport, on the Raritan Bay, was laid out in 1830. It was a flourishing town with schooners, sloops, and steamers landing at the two docks. The inhabitants of the seaport town were occupied in water-related activities—Chingarora oysters were famous, ferryboats and steamers were built in the old yards, and in later years the trade switched to pleasure and speed boats. The townfolk took their pleasure in leisure time activities on the water, and at the Broadway Theatre for the Keyport Yacht Club annual ball. Courtesy of the Monmouth College Library

This souvenir "programme" for the fifth annual Long Branch Carnival in 1913 lists the spectacles to be viewed and the events in which the townspeople might compete. The three days of activities included a parade of businessmen and firemen, coronation of the queen, a doll carnival, a baby parade, bicycle polo, chariot races, and clown acts. Special entertainments were hosted at the hotels for the queen and her court. The brochure also included biographies and pictures of the organizers; lists of parade marshals and judges; and advertisements of local businesses, hotels, and merchants. Courtesy of the Monmouth College Library

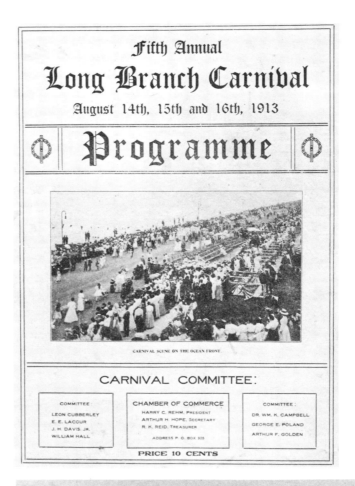

Many knew Geraldine Livingston Thompson as "New Jersey's First Lady," "The Great Lady of Brookdale," "The First Lady of Monmouth County," or just as "Mrs. Thompson." In 1968, a year after Mrs. Thompson's death, and according to the terms of her will, Monmouth County acquired her portion of Brookdale Farm, in Lincroft. At the time of her death on September 9, 1967, Mrs. Thompson could not have known that within a few years Brookdale's great twenty-mare barn would house student learning stations, and the "sick" barn would contain the offices of the president and administrative staff of Brookdale Community College. Courtesy of the *Register*

The entire block between Essex and Sussex avenues, Spring Lake, was purchased in September 1913 and construction was begun on the Essex and Sussex, a 275-room hotel which opened for the 1914 season. The hotel, victim of sheriff's sales, inflation, and foreclosure was open for the 1982 season, but its future is unknown.

Developers want to convert to condominiums, which the local residents are fighting. The Essex and Sussex Hotel provided the early 1900s flavor for the movie *Ragtime;* the hotel was the set for some of the scenes for the 1980 production. Courtesy of the Monmouth College Library

137

On December 26, 1913 the winds whistled through Sea Bright at 123 miles per hour. A few days later, January 3, another winter storm packing winds of 120 miles an hour leveled thirty homes, more than twenty fishermen's shacks, and the Octagon Hotel pictured here. It also flooded and ruined a public street. A third and final storm on February 14 whipped through on winds of 116 miles per hour, making 1913-1914 a memorable winter for the Sea Bright folk. Courtesy of the Moss Archives

In the summer visitors to the summer communities revel in the ocean bathing and the salt air breezes. After September the townsfolk are at the mercy of the moon tides, winds, and storms that follow up along the coast. These close-up photos of the aftermath of the January 3, 1914 storm show the extensive beach erosion and the destruction of the cottages along the beach at Sea Bright. Courtesy of the Moss Archives

138

The fury of the ocean is demonstrated by the damage to the Long Branch and Seashore Railroad tracks on the north beach of Sea Bright. The present sea wall was built along this path incorporating some of the old railroad bulkheading. Courtesy of the Moss Archives

The crew of this Long Branch and Seashore train posed in Sea Bright in 1914. They were (*top*) Hennessey (first name unknown) and Joseph Mahar, and (*bottom*) Henry Tilton and John Rise. Bowser's garage in the background was torn down in 1981 to make way for a drive-in for the Central Jersey Bank. Courtesy of the Moss Archives

Members of Miss Sculthorpe's first grade class at the Branchport School in Long Branch pose for their class picture in 1915. Photo courtesy of Helen Cable

The Pleasure Bay Amusement Park was controlled by the Atlantic Coast Trolley Line which stopped there. The steamboats also docked nearby. There were many hotels in the area where excellent shore dinners were served.

The neighborhood was a popular spot for theatre people—the Barrymores and Drews dined there, and songwriters Charles H. Hoyt, Gus Edwards, and George M. Cohan enjoyed the gaiety and excitement. Tony Pastor's

group came to boat and fish, and Harry Williams was inspired to write "In the Shade of the Old Apple Tree" while staying at the Green Gables Inn in the vicinity. Courtesy of the Monmouth College Library

140

LANDING FROM THE FISHING SCHOONER ASBURY PARK

Prior to World War I, a fishing schooner took passengers for rides off the Asbury Park beach. The passengers were transferred from a landing stage on the fishing pier, or from the beach. The small boat pictured is an example of one type of Sea Bright skiff used for that purpose. The big-hatted and long-skirted women passengers were landed dry shod by the crew. Courtesy of the Monmouth College Library

LAUNCH "WATER WITCH,"
CAPT. B. F. CHAMPION.

Handsome 50 foot Launch, Fitted with all Modern Improvements.

May be Chartered for Pleasure or Fishing. Capacity Twenty Persons.

Full Stock of Soft Drinks on Ice.

ALL DAY, $20.
HALF DAY, $10.
NIGHT, $10.

TELEPHONE CALL:
13-A, ATLANTIC HIGHLANDS.

One could purchase a ticket or two for a lovely Sunday afternoon trip on the Navesink and Shrewsbury rivers, or charter the yacht to view a regatta or to fish. The charter boat business, still very prosperous, had its start in the early 1900s. Courtesy of the Moss Archives

This picture, taken at Shadow Lawn on September 2, 1916, shows President Woodrow Wilson being officially informed of his renomination by the Democratic Party as their candidate for a second presidential term. He made the Shadow Lawn mansion in West Long Branch his summer White House. Senator Ollie James of Kentucky is seen speaking. Photo courtesy of Monmouth College Library

On June 4, 1917 a convoy of army trucks, loaded with equipment and military personnel, lumbered up to Camp Vail at the old abandoned Monmouth Race Track in Little Silver. This trip from New York in the Selden Sixes was historic—for this was the first contingent of troops assigned to the site selected for wartime Signal Corps training. Photo courtesy of the Monmouth College Library

In June 1917, when the war with Germany was two months old, the first troops arrived at Camp Vail. These soldiers, telephone men from New York, became the first Signal Corps soldiers to serve in France during World War I. Courtesy of the Monmouth College Library

142

Camp Alfred Vail was situated on a small peninsula on the South Shrewsbury River. The post was named for the New Jerseyan who was associated with Samuel F. B. Morse. (These men devised the Morse code, the finger key, the automatic roller, and other communications refinements.) In 1917 tents were pitched in the potato fields of Charles Prothero, within sight of the fire-gutted Old Monmouth Race Track. There were 19 cases of poison ivy the first month, 129 the next. Courtesy of the Monmouth College Library

The Red Cross did much to enhance the morale of the troops assigned to Camp Vail. The soldiers themselves managed camp dances and enlisted men's boxing bouts. Courtesy of the Monmouth College Library

Helen Van Benthuysen is crowned Queen of the May at the Branchport School in Long Branch in 1918. Seated, from *left to right,* are Gertrude Ulbrych, Eleanor Sharp, Effie Layton, Delores Burke, an unidentified child, and Clara Whitty. Photo courtesy of Helen Cable

In mid-December 1918 four airplane hangars were built at Camp Vail to accommodate the de Havilands, and the ground was drained and levelled for the construction of two flying fields. The 122nd Aero Squadron Service arrived from Kelly Field, Texas to maintain and repair the aircraft which were used for airplane direction-finding experiments. Courtesy of the Monmouth College Library

World War I veterans gather shortly after the close of the war at a reunion in Freehold. The veterans are, *left to right,* front row: Eugene Reynolds, Clarence Ray, Alex Griffiths, Francis Cahill, Ben Allen, and Fred Mills; middle row: William Carter, Charles Lewis, Harold Stansfield, William Donahue, and John "Scott" Carswell; top row: Joshua Allen, Willare Metzel, Albert Carlson, unknown, Henry Barkalow, and Raymond Jones. Photo courtesy of the Freehold Borough Library

Fort Monmouth served as headquarters of the Carrier Pigeon Service. This photograph, taken shortly after the close of World War I, shows a mobile message center. Photo courtesy of the Newark Public Library

A popular song in the late 1920s was "Asbury Park Down by the Sea" written by John R. Wolter. Photo from the collection of R. Van Benthuysen

145

The indigenous Sea Bright Skiff of Monmouth County attained wide recognition for its performance and seaworthiness during the power boat boom in the 1920s. When adapted for pleasure, the product of one builder, Joseph Banfield, exemplified speed, safety, and good looks. Courtesy of Dr. Peter J. Guthorn

The Brakeley Canning Plant on Manalapan Avenue in Freehold is shown about 1921; the man standing beside the tractor is Joseph Brakeley.

The men on the tractor are unknown. Standing in the background, from *left to right,* are John Powers, Hugh

McGowan, and William M. Smock. Photo courtesy of the Freehold Borough Library

This photo of the Freehold High School baseball team of 1922 was taken on the front porch of Mrs. Parker, who lived on Hudson Street next to the High School. The players are: *front row, left to right,* Meyer Foosaner, John MacMurtrie, Gilday Freeman, Edward King, and Wesley Walling; *second row,* H. John Whitman, coach; Aloysius Carey, Clifford Burke, George Quinn, and Warren McChesney; *third row,* Charles McCue and Brandt Davis. Photo courtesy of the Freehold Borough Library

146

Proud members of the Red Bank Fire Department pose in front of the firehouse on Church Street in the 1920s. Photo courtesy of the Red Bank Public Library

The fancy rig of the Freehold Goodwill Fire Company No. 1 is pictured in front of the firehouse in the 1920s. The man at the steering wheel is unknown, but next to him is John Throckmorton. Photo courtesy of the Freehold Borough Library

In 1923 the Ku Klux Klan met in the Belmar Methodist Church and more than 25,000 gathered from the eastern region for a picnic at Elkwood Park in Oceanport. Many marched down Broadway, Long Branch in full regalia, led by the local contingent of 1,000. In 1925, 7,000 attended a meeting in the Ocean Grove Auditorium. In recent years alarm has spread over the revival of the Klan in Monmouth. Flyers have been found on windshields with the "Save our land. . .join the Klan" theme, and in the past ten years there have been a few fiery confrontations. Courtesy of the Moss Archives

Shark River Hills was only an "auto bus" ride away from the real estate offices of Morrisey and Walker at the Boardwalk and Cookman Avenue in Asbury Park. Lots were offered for as little down as ninety-five dollars, with ten dollars down each month. Those who saw this advertising fan and followed the advice to invest in 1925 saw a 100 percent value increase on their holdings the following year. Courtesy of the Monmouth College Library

OFFICE OF THE
GRAND DRAGON
KNIGHTS OF THE KU KLUX KLAN
REALM OF NEW JERSEY
OFFICIAL DOCUMENT

Vol. 1.   Belmar, New Jersey, November 1, 1926, AK-LX.   No. 9

WHAT THE CATHOLIC CHURCH THINKS OF THE PUBLIC SCHOOLS

Men   Attention--Fiery Summons   Women

You are hereby summoned to an urgent Special Meeting on

Monday, November 1st, 1926, 8 P. M.

at any one of the following places:
ASBURY PARK, Wireless.   LONG BRANCH, Elkwood.
HARMONY, Middletown.

This Call is Important. Wonderful Speakers. Entertainment
Be There for the Safety of Monmouth County

148

This is a truck used by the Van Brunt and Son Trucking Company in the 1920s. Photo courtesy of the Monmouth County Historical Association

Editor, manager, and sole owner of the *Red Bank Register,* John H. Cook was a very aggressive newspaperman. He always fought for what he considered best for Red Bank. In 1928, fifty years after having established the newspaper, he sold his interest. He continued as the paper's editor until his sudden death from a heart attack on January 1, 1930. Photo courtesy of the Red Bank Public Library

Beginning in 1923, Kathryn Stafford organized a weekly children's dancing class during the summer seasons. Children of the cottage colony in Spring Lake, as well as those staying at the hotel could attend. At the end of the summer the class came in costume and presented a pageant for the parents and guests of the Essex and Sussex Hotel in Spring Lake. This picture was taken in the summer of 1926. Courtesy of Jane Grammer

Grace Blackwell is shown boarding an ambulance owned by the Monmouth County Organization for Social Services at the organization's headquarters on Pearl Street, in Red Bank, in 1928. This building was constructed in 1927 and occupied by the organization until 1950. Courtesy of the *Register*

SEA BRIGHT
AIRDROME, Inc.

Phone 196	Box Office Opens 8:00 P. M.
ADMISSION —:— 20c., 35c., 50c.	
Program for the Week of July 22d to July 27th Subject to Change	
Monday July 22	Reginald Denny, Marceline Day in "RED HOT SPEED" Collegians. Comedy, A Woman's Man
Tuesday July 23	Dorothy Sebastian, Larry Kent in "SPIRIT OF YOUTH" "Newlyweds Holiday". Oddities
Weds'day July 24	Corinne Griffith, Victor Varconi in "THE DIVINE LADY" Cameo Comedy. News
Thursday July 25	Ruth Taylor, James Hall in "JUST MARRIED" Comedy. Colored Classics
Friday July 26	Clara Bow in "THE WILD PARTY" Dooley Comedy. Inkwe l
Saturday July 27	Leatrice Joy, Betty Bronson in "THE BELLAMY TRIAL" Gang Comedy, "Election Days". News

The airdrome was the forerunner of today's movie theater. The patrons sat on benches in an area enclosed at the sides but open to the stars. Summer residents were entertained at airdromes in Highland Beach, Sea Bright, and Long Branch. This flyer announced a July weekly program in 1929. Courtesy of the Moss Archives

In the 1920s and 1930s many famous boxers maintained training camps in Monmouth County. In this photograph Gene Tunney trains for an upcoming bout with a youthful sparring partner. Photo courtesy of the Red Bank Public Library

150

In 1929 construction was started on the new north wing of the Essex and Sussex Hotel in Spring Lake. The addition contained seventy-five guest rooms and twenty-five for employees. The cottages facing north on Sussex Avenue, connected by a covered wooden walkway, were leveled. Courtesy of Jane Grammer

After the original Shadow Lawn mansion was destroyed by fire in 1927, the owner, Hubert T. Parson, president of the F. W. Woolworth Company, immediately set about replacing the structure with a fireproof, French-style mansion. He chose, as his architect, Horace Trumbauer of Philadelphia. The 130-room mansion was completed in 1930. It was placed on the National Register of Historic Sites in 1978. Photo courtesy of the Monmouth College Library

John F. Casey's plane parked on the ice of the Navesink River at Red Bank in 1930. Casey owned and operated the Red Bank Airport which began business in 1927; the airport ceased operating in 1971. Photo courtesy of the Red Bank Public Library

151

During the depression of the 1930s many cities that were unable to meet their payrolls issued scrip certificates to employees, entitling them to receive money due them at some future date. This is a sample of scrip issued by the city of Long Branch in 1934. Photo courtesy of the Moss Archives

Surviving crewman of the *Morro Castle* work frantically to saw through the anchor chain. Photo courtesy of Acme Photo Service

One of the major marine disasters of the twentieth century occurred on the morning of September 8, 1934, when the American Ward Line cruise ship *Morro Castle* burned off the Monmouth County coast. Eighty-six passengers and forty-nine crew members died; the ship was a total loss. It came aground a few hundred yards from the Asbury Park Convention Hall, and a weekend crowd is shown viewing the hulk. The ship was hauled off the beach on March 14, 1935, and towed away to a Baltimore shipyard to be cut up for scrap. Photo courtesy of the Monmouth College Library

152

Here exhausted survivors from the *Morro Castle* disaster are being carried to a Spring Lake bathhouse. First-aid squads from more than a dozen Monmouth County communities assisted in resuscitating those overcome by smoke or exposure. Photo courtesy of the Monmouth College Library

Now the Monmouth Beach headquarters of the New Jersey Marine Police, this structure is one of the few extant United States Coast Guard stations. Amphibious "ducks" were garaged here and used for the evacuation and rescue of local residents during high tides. Courtesy of the Monmouth College Library

OCEAN AVENUE SHOWING U. S. COAST GUARD, MONMOUTH BEACH, N. J.

The community Christmas sing is an annual event in West Long Branch. The first borough Christmas tree was erected in 1916. For many years the tree stood in the center of the road at the intersection of Cedar and Locust avenues. As the volume of traffic increased over the years the tree created a hazard. It is now erected in Woolley Park, just to the east of the intersection. The community sing is held each year on the Sunday before Christmas. This photograph was taken in the 1930s. Photo courtesy of the West Long Branch Historical Society

153

Boat transportation between New York City and Monmouth County was a relief from ordinary train travel. The steamers *Monmouth* and *Sandy Hook* connected with the Jersey Central Railroad trains at Atlantic Highlands, providing transportation as far as Bay Head. Only a summer service, it was not re-established after World War II. Courtesy of the Monmouth College Library

The New Jersey Central railroad built a pier at Atlantic Highlands in 1882; in that year the old railroad terminal at Sandy Hook was abandoned. At the time of this advertisement, the *Monmouth,* built in 1888, had been on the Sandy Hook run since 1889. The *Sandy Hook,* which had also sailed since 1889, was later used by the Army to transport troops in New York from 1942 to 1943. She discontinued service in 1947. Courtesy of the Moss Archives

One of the earliest names associated with Monmouth County boatbuilding and the history of the Sea Skiff was Seaman. The first of the line was Isaac, followed by Walter A., William A., and finally Harold L. Seaman, builders and innovators for a century. The Seaman family originated the name "Sea Skiff" in their advertisements as early as 1875. A page from their catalog just prior to World War II shows their product and prices. Courtesy of Dr. Peter J. Guthorn.

SEAMAN SEA BRIGHT SEA SKIFFS

The choice of PROFESSIONAL DEEP SEA FISHERMEN since their origination at "NAUVOO" (now SEA BRIGHT, N. J.) by Walter A. Seaman in 1841

● Owing to their lightness, stability, surf-carrying capacity, and their ability to land through the surf and skid out on the beach and sit upright when aground they are ideal for tenders, life-boats, bathing-beach rescue-boats, cargo-boats, lighters or any other use requiring exceptional sea-boats capable of carrying exceptional loads through the SURF.

We have reports of 21 footers landing over 5,800 pounds of fish through the surf and 20,000 pounds is not exceptional for the 32 footers. These boats are pulled out of the surf on rollers with their load and stand up under this treatment year after year.

36' x 11' SEA-SKIFF POUND-BOAT
Used by Pound-net Fishermen for use off and on the beach through the surf.

Overhang stern with fishermans Rudder   Regular stern with fishermans Rudder

36' x 11' SEA-SKIFF
(Pound - Net Boat)

STANDARD SIZES

Overhang Stern		Regular Stern
$ 590.	16'x5'	$ 490.
690.	18'x6'	590.
790.	21'x6'9"	690.
990.	26'x8'	890.
1,890.	32'x11'	1,690.
2,190.	36'x11'	1,990.

PRICES ARE for complete Skiffs (as cuts) ready to receive power.

WE INSTALL any make of motor or equipment desired at the prevailing prices.

PRICES ARE subject to change without notice. Orders are accepted contingent upon strikes, fires, accidents, delays by carriers or any cause beyond our control.

21' REGULATION SEA-SKIFF
Used by Professional fishermen for use off and on the beach through the surf.

TELEPHONE L. B. 3495   *Seaman Sea-Skiffs*   LONG BRANCH, N. J.

1841 — PIONEER BUILDERS OF THE FAMOUS SEA BRIGHT SEA - SKIFF — To Date

154

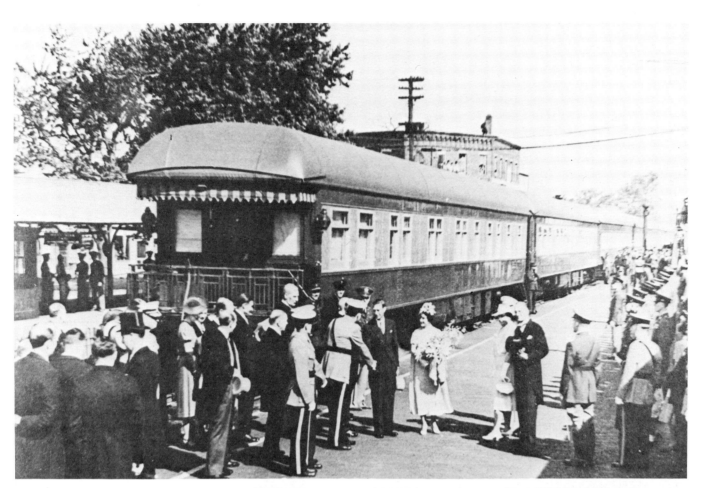

Five silver and blue railroad cars arrived in Red Bank in June 1939. King George VI and Queen Elizabeth were en route from Washington to the World's Fair in Flushing Meadows, Long Island. The royal couple were greeted by Governor A. Harry Moore; the Mayor of Red Bank, Charles R. English; and Mrs. English. The superintendent of the New Jersey State Police was in charge of security. It is said that the crowd that gathered to greet the king and queen numbered 50,000. Courtesy of the *Register*

Alexander Woolcott, the well-known drama critic and radio personality, was born at the site of the North American Phalanx. His grandfather had helped found the socialistic community. It was no longer this by the time Alexander was born, and all that was left was the eighty-five room building where his mother, Frances Grey (Bucklin) Woollcott, gave birth to him on January 19, 1887. Photo courtesy of Monmouth College Library .

Soldiers at Fort Hancock at the start of World War II ride on a railroad line built by the Works Progress Administration. Not only were the railroad lines built by WPA workers, but the WPA also overhauled and rebuilt all the fort's rolling stock. Photo courtesy of the Newark Public Library

Private Andrew Vanyo of Newark sends out a pigeon with a message during a training session at the Army Carrier Pigeon Center at Fort Monmouth in 1941. Photo courtesy of the Newark Public Library

156

Curious bystanders watch Army troops leap over a boardwalk rail in practice repulse of a mock invasion at Asbury Park in 1942. Note the rolled up dimout curtains ready for night use to black out boardwalk lights from the sight of enemy submarines. Photo courtesy of the Newark Public Library

Sunbathers on the beach at Asbury Park in 1942 casually watch as Army troops carry on maneuvers near the city's Convention Hall. Photo courtesy of the Newark Public Library

157

Fred Lange is pictured seated in a 1903 Cadillac that is parked next to a 1942 Cadillac on the Stillwell's Corner farm in Freehold. Photo courtesy of the Freehold Borough Library

William J. Martin, Junior was an *Asbury Park Press* weatherman who continued his father's recordkeeping after his father's death. For fifty-six years the notations were made hourly, twenty-four hours a day, by the father and son. The elder Martin established Long Branch's first official U.S. Weather Bureau in 1896, operating from the telephone building on Broadway and also from his home. William J. Martin, Junior also maintained storm warning centers at the National Guard Armory in Long Branch and the Atlantic Highlands Marine Basin; he operated a center at the North Long Branch pier to test water temperature and salinity, and to mark currents and wave heights. Courtesy of the Monmouth College Library

The sale of Government Bonds was a means of supporting the war effort during World War II. Shown is a bond sales booth in Red Bank in the 1940s. Pictured *left to right* are: Allaire Cornwell, Mayor Charles English, Bill Fluhr, Edward Conway, Jim Humphrey, and Bill Bradley. The identities of the women in the booth are unknown. Photo courtesy of the Red Bank Public Library

158

DEFENSE PARADE
Ocean Ave.
-: SEA BRIGHT :-

Thurs. Evening : July 3d
6 P. M. SHARP

STARTS AT NORTH SEA BRIGHT BEACH
MARCH THROUGH SEA BRIGHT
DISBANDING AT SURF BATHING PAVILION

Kindly Display All
AMERICAN FLAGS
Sea Bright Residents Welcome
In Parade

★ Assist U. S. O. Drive ★

M. H. Robinson, Chairman   Walter J. Sweeney, Mayor

Sea Bright was made more aware of the conflict abroad by the presence of troops guarding her beaches against threatened U-boat attacks and landings. This parade held on the eve of the Fourth of July was for the benefit of the U.S.O., the organization which helped to make the lives of the soldiers quartered in the area more agreeable. Courtesy of the Monmouth College Library

These nurses, representing branches of the armed forces during World War II, were involved in a recruitment drive for nursing students at Fitkin Memorial Hospital; the hospital, located in Neptune, has changed its name to the Jersey Shore Medical Center. Photo courtesy of the Ann May School of Nursing

In October 1942 William Bullock and Elmer Kline of the Allenhurst Line Department of the Jersey Central Power and Light Company were doing their part in salvaging wire and metal. Everyone at home wanted to "get in the scrap" and nothing was too small for the World War II effort. Courtesy of the Monmouth College Library

159

A destructive storm rocked the Monmouth County shore area in September, 1944, and the Asbury Park boardwalk suffered heavy damage. Here a Coast Guardsman patrols the area to protect stores from looters. This view is from the south end of the Asbury Park boardwalk near the Ocean Grove line. Photo courtesy of Mrs. Helen Cable

A hurricane ran up the coast leaving millions of dollars worth of damage in its wake on September 14, 1944. This twisted wreckage of the merry-go-round on the Long Branch pier is testimony to the power of the winds. Courtesy of the Moss Archives

160

Edmund Wilson, the American literary critic and journalist, was born on May 8, 1895 in Red Bank, the only child of Edmund and Helen Mather (Kimball) Wilson. His father was a successful local lawyer and served for several years as attorney general for the state of New Jersey. Critics have suggested that Wilson's best-selling novel *Memoirs of Hecate County* is set in Monmouth County. Photo courtesy of the Monmouth College Library

On January 10, 1946 the U.S. Signal Corps' Diana radar transmitted signals to be reflected off the moon. This was the first contact made outside the earth's atmosphere and heralded outer space communications and flight programs. Scientists and engineers gathered at a shack on Marconi Road in West Belmar. At moonrise, radio waves traveling 186,000 miles a second were sent every four seconds through the Diana's transmitter named Diana (after the mythological huntress and goddess of the moon). Courtesy of the Monmouth College Library

Monmouth's New Image:

1946-1983

In January 1946, bouncing signals off the moon from the Camp Evans area of Fort Monmouth ushered in a new age for Monmouth County, the United States, and the world. The emphasis for many living in Monmouth County would be on space and space communications. The major employers, Fort Monmouth and Bell Laboratories, Holmdel, are engaged in these pursuits, and their presence has attracted similar industries and trained personnel.

Because Monmouth County is in a race with many other areas of the country for high technology industries, the two institutions of higher education in the county, Monmouth College and Brookdale Community College, have increased their offerings in computer science. With firms like Bell Laboratories and Perkin Elmer calling the county home, Monmouth's image is constantly cast in the mold of circuit breakers and silicon chips.

The economy is also bolstered by racing. Horse racing pumps millions of dollars each year into the state treasury and into the local economy. The first race at the new Monmouth Park took place on June 19, 1946. Each year the daily and seasonal influx of visitors to the park and the Freehold Raceway helps to support the restaurant, hotel, and motel trade in the area. The horse breeding population has grown steadily since the 1950s with an increase in hobby farms and those supplying horses for the two tracks.

Horse breeding also helps preserve the open spaces in the county. Upper Freehold, Millstone, Freehold, Manalapan, and Howell townships still have great expanses of open land, but the number of farms that have been turned into housing developments, shopping malls, and industrial complexes has reduced farmland by 61,934 acres. In spite of declining farmlands, Monmouth County is still ranked first in production of soybeans and cabbage, and has the greatest number of certified nurseries in New Jersey.

The completion of new highways also stimulated the Monmouth County economy. The Garden State Parkway, constructed in the early 1950s, revitalized the tourist trade. In the 1970s $400 million or 8.6% of all income, was derived from tourism. Beaches, parks, and amusement areas are now within a few hours' drive and the public appears to be opting for visits to shore resorts rather than more extended, expensive vacations.

The Deserted Village at Allaire, used by the Army during World War II for target practice, opened as Allaire State Park in 1957. The park added the dimension of "living history" to the ways in which tourists might be entertained.

In 1961 Secretary of the Interior Udall dedicated 460 acres of federal land on the Sandy Hook peninsula for recreational purposes; Sandy Hook State Park opened its beaches in 1962. The park came under federal management in 1974, becoming part of the largest urban

park system, the Gateway National Recreation Area. The National Park Service rangers have developed an extensive educational and environmental program. In 1975 Fort Hancock was deactivated and the buildings and other structures became the basis of the park's interpretive history projects. The history projects are: a house refurbished on Officer's Row to reflect turn of the century living—a reenacted sea rescue with Lyle gun and breeches buoy—show and tell at the batteries (fortifications)—ethnic fairs, nineteenth century farming methods, and talks and tours which proceed from the museum.

The recently completed highways, Route 18 and I-195, led to residential and industrial development; land was opened in the outlying areas. The land values were so high and the pressure so great that the farmers were unable to resist selling their land. The strength of the "save the farm" movement of the 1980s comes from the new residents who want to live "on the farm" in the city. Multiple dwellings, once rare in the county, make up more than one-third of the new housing, especially along the coastal areas.

Fishing has declined over the years; fish populations have been reduced by dumping and the con-

Volunteer first aid squads provide an important service for the residents of Monmouth County; most of the fifty-three municipalities in the county have their own squads. Pictured, in 1952, are Walter Luebben and Robert Searby, members of the Freehold First Aid Squad; Searby was president at the time. Photo courtesy of the Newark Public Library

struction of new sewage plants. Though the big commercial fishermen are catching more fish today and making more money, the baymen and inshore boatmen are not so prosperous. Local fishermen are no longer able to sell their excess catches to Seacoast Products, Incorporated, once Middletown's largest industry. For seventy-five years the company harvested menhaden for fish oil, margarine, ink, soap, and paint, and for fish meal for hog and poultry feed. Then in 1973 Seacoast was purchased by a London holding company and closed. Plans to build a fish processing factory and clam depuration facility are expected to take up the slack.

The clammers have also had their problems. In the early 1970s clam beds on the bay shore were lost to pollution, until a depuration plant was started in 1974. Today

164

In 1953 a war memorial was unveiled in Middletown by Marine Staff Sergeant Richard Dwyer and WAC Lieutenant Dorothy Watson. Photo courtesy of the Newark Public Library

customers agree that the clams are pure and sand-free.

Monmouth County farmers still manage to make ends meet, but it is a struggle. Vegetable and fruit growers continue to reap a good yield and Monmouth County farmers grow a little bit of almost everything. Monmouth ranks second in the state for over-all agricultural production and is number one in the production of potatoes. In addition, Monmouth ranks second in the state for sweet corn yield and third in apples, according to New Jersey agricultural statistics. In a different market Monmouth County is the leader in nursery stock, dedicating "well over 4,000 acres" to the production of young trees and foliage.

Monmouth County is situated midway along the Boston-Washington megalopolis. The ratables in the county are being projected to rise more than $13 million by the end of this decade. The heaviest growth areas for the future are estimated to be Eatontown and Red Bank, Freehold, Middletown, Howell, and Manalapan townships. Foreign companies have invested in Monmouth County because of the large labor pool and the proximity of road and rail networks to the larger transportation centers.

The growing labor force has helped bring both manufacturing and service industries to the county. The electrical machinery industry has been the leading employer for many years. Apparel, glass, and

chemical production are next in importance. The largest employer in the county is Fort Monmouth, where 2,000 military personnel and 7,700 civilians are employed. The largest industrial employer in the county is Bell Laboratories with more than 4,000 people on the payroll. These scientific and technical people, along with the engineering and scientific personnel employed at permanent military installations contribute to the highly educated quality of the population. Skilled labor is partly a product of the county's vocational training schools whose programs span twenty-one occupations.

The county's population has more than doubled in the last thirty years. The decade of the 1970s saw an influx of Asians; they are the newest minority at the shore, mostly casualties of the Vietnam War. The Cossacks in Howell Township brought many Kalmuks here in the 1950s; they had been living in European refugee camps since World War II. The smallest group is the American Indian. Blacks make up 8.5 percent of the population; the largest community is in Neptune Township. Long Branch and Middletown have the

165

largest enclaves of Spanish-speaking people; 30,000 live in the city. From 1967-1970 there were riots among the Blacks in Red Bank, Long Branch, and Asbury Park. Gangs of youths roamed the business districts fire bombing and looting. Asbury Park suffered the worst destruction and was declared a disaster area by Governor William Cahill. The youths were calling attention to their needs for better housing, recreation, and jobs.

During the period from 1946 to 1983, a number of events in Monmouth County gained statewide and nationwide attention. In 1954 Junior Senator Joseph R. McCarthy and his Senate investigation team turned their attention to Fort Monmouth. Thirty-five employees, mostly engineers, were suspended as a result of the televised hearings that accused the Army of "coddling communists" and permitting a spy ring to operate.

Monmouth County again made media headlines in 1958 when eight Nike Ajax missiles exploded at the Chapel Hill, Middletown base. Six soldiers and four civilians died in the mishap.

In 1966 one of the most sensational trials in the nation spotlighted Freehold, the county seat. Dr. Carl Coppolino, a Red Bank anesthesiologist, was acquitted of the murder of Colonel William E. Farber and within a year was convicted of the second-degree murder of his first wife in Naples, Florida. F. Lee Bailey, famous Boston attorney, defended Coppolino.

Joseph Valachi, a New York narcotics peddler, became a star witness for Senator McClellan's crime and narcotics investigations. Valachi was placed under heavy guard at Fort Monmouth during this time. Corruption in Monmouth County, particularly Long Branch, became the object of state and local probes as a result of these hearings.

Monmouth College, the county's first institution of higher learning,

began as a junior college in 1933; the Long Branch High School classrooms were used after 4:00 p.m. In 1956 Monmouth Junior College moved to the Shadow Lawn estate in West Long Branch. Since 1958 more than 11,000 baccalaureate and 1,800 graduate degrees have been conferred.

Geraldine Thompson's farm Brookdale, the breeding and training ground for Derby winner "Regret," became the site of the county's community college in 1968. The hundred-year-old barns have been adapted for educational purposes and new buildings have been constructed in the barn mode; the campus retains its very rural setting.

Movie-making returned to the shore when Woody Allen's *Stardust Memories* was filmed in Ocean

Grove and Belmar in the summer of 1980; *Ragtime* used the elegant Essex and Sussex Hotel in Spring Lake to convey the flavor of 1906; and Daddy Warbucks and family moved into the Shadow Lawn mansion in West Long Branch for the filming of *Annie* in the spring of 1981.

Perhaps the most spectacular event of this period, from 1946 to 1983, was in 1976 with the lineup of tall ships in Sandy Hook Bay for our country's 200th birthday. Countries around the world, most of which had populated Monmouth County, sent their sailing ships as their contribution to the celebration of our Bicentennial, and almost every municipality in Monmouth County staged a parade or historical festivity. ●

This 1950s photo shows Edward Feltus, the late director of the Monmouth County Historical Association, with an unidentified soldier using a mine detector. They were searching for buried cannons at the site of the Battle of Monmouth. Photo courtesy of the Monmouth County Historical Association

Kathryn Elkus White, three-term mayor of Red Bank, is seen talking to a friend on Broad Street in September 1954. Mrs. White subsequently served as acting state treasurer and as chairman of the New Jersey Highway Authority, and was instrumental in the development of the New Jersey Department of Community Affairs. Involved in community, state, and national affairs, Mrs. White proved that the roles of wife and mother could be combined with a career. Courtesy of the *Register*

The Garden State Parkway is a limited access toll road running through the eastern portion of Monmouth County. Its completion, in 1954, made the county more accessible to North Jersey, increased the number of summer tourists, and brought in more year-round residents. A glance at population increase figures, relocations of industries, and the influx of summer visitors tells the story of the impact the parkway has had on the area. Photo from the collection of R. Van Benthuysen

In 1945 a nucleus of engineers and scientists recently discharged from the Signal Corps started Electronic Associates. The company has since grown to a group of over 800 associates. From a small store-like building in the West End section of Long Branch, the firm has grown to a major position in the field of electronics, EAI products are marketed worldwide to the aerospace, electric power, and other energy-related industries. The firm's modern administrative center and manufacturing plant opened in West Long Branch in 1958. Photo courtesy of Charles H. Maps, Junior

168

In 1958 Mayor J. Owen Woolley of West Long Branch spoke at the opening of the Electronic Associates administrative headquarters and manufacturing plant located on Highway 36 in his community. Photo courtesy of the Monmouth College Library

In 1876 the Monmouth Hotel was built in Spring Lake on land that had been patented by Robert H. Morris in 1770. The first cottage on this site had been constructed in 1870 for a Presbyterian minister, Reverend A. A. Willett. With its 250 rooms the old hotel had accommodations for 500 guests, and with the addition of a new wing the number of rooms increased to 386. The main building was 310 feet by 46 feet and the wing was 150 feet by 46 feet. The dining room alone, where fancy balls and parties were held, was 50 feet by 111 feet. On September 19, 1900 the hotel was burned with two others and eight cottages; it was rebuilt in 1904, and catered to an elite clientele until 1974. Today a housing development stands in its place. Courtesy of the Monmouth College Library

Buck Engineering Company was started in Freehold during 1934. In the late 1950s it developed and successfully introduced a line of basic instruments for high school physical science programs. The firm now occupies a modern building in Wall Township. Office, laboratory, engineering, production, and warehousing operations are all consolidated in one building. Courtesy of the *Register*

169

The American Hotel in Freehold is a popular place for class reunions. Pictured are members of the Freehold High School class of 1910 at their fiftieth reunion. Seated from *left to right* are: Marion Hance DuBois, Druscilla Okerson Morris, Georgia Lockwood Markle, unidentified, Edith Thompson Branford, and Helen Stillwell Brown. Standing, from *left to right* are an unidentified lady, Marion Davison, Julius E. Dittmar, David Baird, another unidentified lady, and Nora Clayton. Photo courtesy of the Freehold Borough Library

In 1961 a student, Bruce Frankel of Wanamassa, was instrumental in having a marker placed at the site where President Garfield died on September 19, 1881. Daniel Ardolino, president of the Long Branch Monument Company, donated his services toward the project. Photo courtesy of the Newark Public Library

Bell Laboratories Center for Telecommunications Development in Holmdel is a six-story, glass enclosed building designed by the famous architect, the late Eero Saarinen. The building stands on a 486-acre plot and was completed in 1963. The Holmdel facility also acts as Bell Laboratories' quality assurance center. Researchers there continually test equipment used in the Bell System to make sure it meets standards intended by the designer. Bell Laboratories scientists at Holmdel were involved with the Echo and Telstar satellite research during the early 1960s. Courtesy of the *Register*

Kathryn Elkus White of Red Bank was appointed the United States' ambassador to Denmark in 1964. She is seen here with her husband, Arthur J. White, and the King of Denmark. Mrs. White's father, Abram I. Elkus, was ambassador to Turkey during the administration of Woodrow Wilson. Courtesy of the *Register*

What appears to be a picture of the back dunes at Sandy Hook is actually a picture of a Nike site. The missiles, buried in their silos, were rarely seen in their raised strike position. In January 1964 the First Battalion of the Fifty-first Air Defense Artillery manned this Nike Hercules battery. As a result of a Pentagon drive to save money, in the spring of 1974 the firing battery began deactivation; the procedure was completed in October 1974. Today the base is abandoned to bayberry bushes, poison ivy, and prickly pear cactus. Courtesy of the Gateway National Recreation Area, Sandy Hook Unit

USS LST-1032 was assigned her name on July 1, 1955; USS *Monmouth County*. Her keel was laid in the Boston Naval Shipyard in June of 1944, and a month later the tank landing ship was launched. the *Monmouth County* beached troops and equipment at Iwo Jima, Okinawa, Saipan, and the Philippines. After the hostilities the ship transported occupation forces to Japan and finally brought the veterans home to San Francisco.

In 1946 the ship became part of the amphibious force of the U.S. Atlantic Fleet and did a stint as a training vessel at Norfolk, Virginia and for various naval reserve units. The vessel returned to the Pacific Fleet in 1966, and as one

of five ships in Landing Squadron 2, operated in the Mekong Delta. The 328-foot ship, which carried a complement of ten officers and eighty-nine enlisted personnel, was decommis-

sioned in 1970. During her active service, the USS *Monmouth County* had been awarded several ship's ribbons and eight bronze stars. Courtesy of the Monmouth College Library

171

Bruce Springsteen, singer, songwriter, and guitarist was born in Freehold on September 23, 1949. His first album was entitled "Greetings from Asbury Park, New Jersey." His song, "Born to Run," which won the Golden Record award in 1975, was nominated as the New Jersey state song. Springsteen performs in New York and New Jersey clubs and is known to drop in and jam at the local clubs. In 1966 Springsteen (on guitar) and Clarence Clemmons (on the baritone saxophone), backed up by the E Street Band, appeared at the Monmouth Arts Center, Red Bank. Courtesy of the *Register*

The Freehold Raceway, the oldest parimutuel harness track in America, dates back to 1853, when it was established by the Monmouth County Agricultural Society. This was during a period when Freehold was strictly an agricultural area. In 1966 the racing plant was renovated. The old track, wide enough for only six horses, was widened to eighty feet and purse money was increased. Soon the nation's top horses and drivers began racing at Freehold regularly, and records began to topple. Courtesy of the *Register*

172

Brookdale, the County College of Monmouth, is set in the rural atmosphere of a 225-acre former horse farm that was formerly the property of Geraldine Livingston Thompson. The handsome old barns and rambling new buildings fit neatly into the rolling fields and woods of the campus. The college was founded in 1967 and enrolled its first class on the Lincroft campus in the fall of 1969. One adjunct center, two community learning centers, and a large number of extension centers are operated by Brookdale to bring its programs to the community. Courtesy of the *Register*

This modern addition to the Murry and Leonie Guggenheim Memorial Library of Monmouth College was dedicated in 1968. Funding for the addition was provided by the Guggenheim Foundation and the federal government. The library serves as a depository for state and federal documents and maintains a special collection dealing with the history of the North Jersey shore area. Bernard Grad and Son, of Newark, were the architects for the addition. Courtesy of the Monmouth College Publications Office

173

In October 1968 the Monmouth County Library opened its Eastern Branch in Shrewsbury. The adult reading area can be converted into a concert hall by the removal of tables and roll-away shelving. Grants from various federal and state agencies have funded popular, jazz, ensemble, and orchestral concerts. Flanking the mezzanine stairway (below) are members of the Monmouth Civic Chorus in Christmas concert. At right a jazz ensemble livens up a library meeting room. Courtesy of the Monmouth County Library

In celebration of the one hundredth anniversary of the Liberty Grange in Marlboro, the building was renovated by members in 1975. However, despite its widespread social and economic service in the area, the Liberty Grange, like other granges in the area, has gradually lost many of its members. The remaining active members place the blame on today's fast-paced highly technological world for the Grange's current small active membership. Photo from the collection of R. Van Benthuysen

The *Alexander Hamilton*, a Hudson River dayliner and one of the last side-wheelers, was floated to the old steamer dock in Atlantic Highlands in the mid 1970s. The Alexander Hamilton Society has anticipated restoring the ship with boutiques and a restaurant. The ship lies in the mud now off the Earle Ammunition Depot pier, with only her stacks visible above the water. Courtesy of the *Register*

In 1976 the Kalmuk residents of Howell Township finished building this smaller version of the Golden Pavilion built by Chinese craftsmen for the 1930 World's Fair in Chicago. The people, refugees from Kalmuk, U.S.S.R., were casualties of World War II. Many came to the United States—some to Howell in Monmouth, others to Philadelphia and Vineland, New Jersey. The ancestors of these Kalmuks came from the East—China, Japan, and Korea, and brought Buddhism to Russia. They accept Buddha as a divine savior. Courtesy of the *Register*

All the fifty-three municipalities in Monmouth County had ceremonies to mark the Bicentennial. This photograph shows a parade in progress in Shrewsbury; the Quaker meetinghouse is in the background. Photo courtesy of the Shrewsbury Historical Society

176

On June 13, 1976, the new Temple Beth El Synagogue on Monmouth Road in Ocean Township was dedicated. Its modern architecture immediately made it one of the outstanding landmarks in the township. Temple Beth El has a membership of close to 300 families, several of which have been associated with the temple since its establishment in Asbury Park over a half century ago. Most of the members currently live in Ocean Township, Deal, and surrounding areas. Photo from the collection of R. Van Benthuysen

177

Mrs. William (Brinley) Berner, *left,* unveils a plaque dedicating the Old Free Church Cemetery in West Long Branch. Assisting her is Anita Fornino. This dedication was part of the borough's Bicentennial celebration. Photo courtesy of the West Long Branch Historical Society

A Monmouth County Viking throwback was produced by Keyport boatbuilders Erik and Ivan Pederson. In place of their usual modern Sea Bright Skiff, a replica of a Viking long ship was conceived and designed by the brothers. The thirty-foot version, christened *Valhalla,* reviewed Operation Sail's 1976 gathering of tall ships in Sandy Hook Bay. Courtesy of the *Register*

The Congregation Brothers of Israel, the Jewish orthodox congregation of Long Branch, recently moved from its Second Avenue site in downtown Long Branch to the Elberon section of the city. In the 1960s the congregation began to feel pressed for more spacious quarters closer to the majority of its congregants. On March 27, 1977, a parade of congregants and guests carrying Torahs and ornaments proceeded from the old building to the new synagogue on Park Avenue in Elberon. Photo from the collection of R. Van Benthuysen

Morris Metterman, a Holocaust survivor, settled on a chicken farm in Howell Township following World War II. He is shown here in his egg packing room. When Mr. Metterman died in November, 1979 his wife closed the farm down. Photo courtesy of Rita Nannini

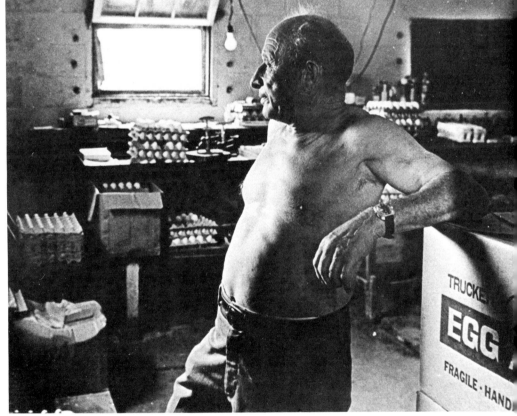

179

It is traditional for many of the volunteer fire companies in Monmouth County to hold fairs or carnivals during the summer. These provide a means of raising funds, but equally important, these affairs serve as community gatherings where old friends meet to chat while their children ride ponies, eat cotton candy, and attempt to win prizes offered by games of skill. Typical of these fairs is that held by the Colts Neck Fire Department. George Illmensee, Junior, chairman of the fair, and Joseph Wilson, right, fair adviser, supervised the preparations for the week-long fair in 1978. One of the displays that year was a 1923 Ahrens-Fox fire engine. Courtesy of the *Register*

Dr. Robert W. Wilson and Dr. Arno Penzias, engineers assigned to the Bell Laboratories in Holmdel, were the 1978 Nobel Prize winners for physics. They were awarded the prize for research conducted on the cosmic background of radiation. Their work provided conclusive evidence to support the theory that the universe was created by a cataclysmic explosion, or "big bang." Dr. Wilson is a resident of Holmdel Township. Courtesy of the *Register*

Monmouth College acquired its present campus in West Long Branch in 1956 when it purchased the Shadow Lawn estate. Since acquiring the estate the college has undertaken an extensive building program that includes a gymnasium, several modern classroom buildings, and a College Center. Photo courtesy of the Monmouth College Publications Office

180

This view shows the colonnade area adjoining the formal gardens at the Shadow Lawn estate, Monmouth College. Ralph Binder photo

A May commencement day at Monmouth College is shown. In the background is Woodrow Wilson Hall, the college's administration building. Ralph Binder photo

Dr. Samuel H. Magill became the fifth president of Monmouth College in 1980. Previously Dr. Magill had been president of Simon's Rock Early College in Great Barrington, Massachusetts. Magill, a graduate of the University of North Carolina at Chapel Hill, received a bachelor of divinity degree from Yale University and a doctorate from Duke University. Photo courtesy of the Office of Editorial Services, Monmouth College

The First United Methodist Church on Monmouth Road in Oakhurst has this eye-catching sign to attract worshippers. Photo from the collection of R. Van Benthuysen

182

INTERIOR AUDITORIUM, SHOWING THE LARGEST ORGAN IN THE WORLD, OCEAN GROVE, N.J.

Ocean Grove was established as a place for camp meetings by the Methodist Church. Until a few years ago automobile traffic was prohibited on Sunday. Initially a summer community, it gradually has become an all-year community. Its auditorium, with a famous organ, has a full summer program of great religious leaders, outstanding orators, and famous musicians. Courtesy of the Monmouth College Library

Max Tannenbaum, a retired egg farmer, is shown teaching Hebrew to a Bar Mitzvah student at the Farmingdale Synagogue in 1980. Photo courtesy of Rita Nannini

183

These two scenes taken at a recent Monmouth County Fair illustrate the interest that the youth of the county show in farming. Working with an 1890s corn sheller are Paul Scotese, Holmdel and Shelly Huber, of Middletown. Nancy O'Connell of Oceanport helps farmer John Snyder grade potatoes according to size. Courtesy of the *Register*

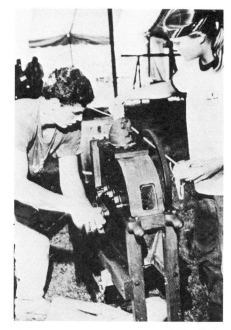

Mr. and Mrs. Fred Green of Farmingdale are shown at the sales counter of their retail sales room. Most of the chicken farmers in the Howell-Farmingdale area who remain active today are so because they have established a retail trade. Photo courtesy of Rita Nannini

Mr. Green holding one of his chickens, 1982. Photo courtesy of Rita Nannini

Delicious Orchards in Colts Neck began operating in 1910. Today, besides growing, harvesting, and selling apples to retail stores, the 200-acre orchard also produces cider and baked goods, which the owners sell at their own retail store on the premises. From modest beginnings, the owners have added full lines of cheese, vegetables, other fruits, and specialty items during the sixteen-year existence of the store. Photo from the collection of R. Van Benthuysen

An important source of farm income was the conversion of grain or fruit to distilled spirits. It was a product which did not deteriorate with age but actually improved. The large local apple crop was used to produce "apple jack" beginning in the Colonial period. A pioneer, Robert Laird of Scobeyville, established a distillery in 1780. It is carried on by his descendants. Courtesy of the *Register*

Fishing, carried out by inshore gill netting and offshore "dragging" continues as a Monmouth County industry. The owners of these ships are members of the Belford Seafood Cooperative Association which processes and markets the fish. Fresh fish is available at a market run by the cooperative on Main Street. Courtesy of Jane Grammer

185

After 134 years in the same premises on route 537, the Colts Neck General Store is still a success in these days of big, modern supermarkets. The owners have preserved the outside of the building with its open porch, turned railings, and hitching posts. Photo from the collection of R. Van Benthuysen

This drawing shows the administrative offices of the Shadow Lawn Savings and Loan Company located in West Long Branch; the building was dedicated in 1981. Photo courtesy of Shadow Lawn Savings and Loan Company

186

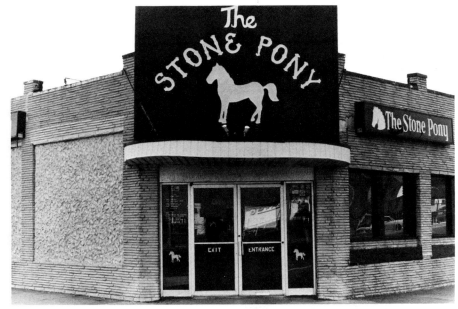

The Stone Pony on Ocean Avenue in Asbury Park is where the rock group called Southside Johnny and the Asbury Jukes got their start; Bruce Springsteen has also appeared at the Stone Pony. Photo from the collection of R. Van Benthuysen

Bluegrass, which had its origins in Appalachia in the eighteenth century, stars at the Englishtown Music Hall at 24 Water Street in Englishtown. The hall, which opened in 1975, was almost completely destroyed by fire in June 1977, but reopened the following April. The programs include country and bluegrass music, clog dancing exhibitions, and children's bluegrass programs. Funded by the Eastern Education Network, the program "Bluegrass at the Englishtown Music Hall" was taped in 1977 for New Jersey Public Television. Courtesy of the *Register*

This sign shows Monmouth County's ethnic diversity. This kosher pizza parlor is located on Norwood Avenue in Deal. Photo from the collection of R. Van Benthuysen

187

The International Flavors and Fragrances Company is a leading producer of flavor and fragrance compounds used in a wide variety of consumer products. The company has manufacturing plants in Union Beach and in the neighboring community of Hazlet, both in Monmouth County. Courtesy of the *Register*

The computer systems division of the Perkin Elmer Corporation is located on a thirty-acre site in Oceanport; it employs 1,300 people at this plant. Perkin Elmer is a $1 billion Fortune 500 corporation. Courtesy of the *Register*

The Brockway Glass Company, a manufacturer of glass containers, has a plant in Freehold where it employs 800 people. Photo courtesy of the Newark Public Library

188

The ecology-oriented Midland Glass Company is a leader in recycling discarded bottles. However, the company's neighbors in Aberdeen Township contend that Midland is polluting the area with a dangerous, cancer-causing dust. The township council and the New Jersey Department of Environmental Protection are caught between the company and its employees and the residents of the township. Courtesy of the *Register*

The Monmouth County Park System was created by the Board of Chosen Freeholders in 1961. The parks are open 365 days a year and offer family activities, instructional clinics, contests, and tournaments and concerts. At Thompson Park these individuals are learning to ski on specially constructed mats. Courtesy of the *Register*

Amusements parks have been busy attractions during the summer months. Largely patronized by residents from the northern metropolitan areas, transportation was provided by railroad excursions prior to the wide use of the automobile. Parks were situated along the shore of the Raritan Bay, the major rivers, and the ocean front. Day-trippers crowded the parks at Keansburg, Highlands, Pleasure Bay, and the ocean front at Long Branch and Asbury Park. Keansburg (pictured here in the summer of 1982), Long Branch, and Asbury Park still compete for the summer vacationers. Courtesy of the *Register*

This 1982 aerial view shows ocean bathing area I and the visitors center at the Sandy Hook Unit of Gateway National Recreation area. Clearly it is either a beautiful summer weekday or very early on a weekend morning. Beach erosion due to this past winter's high tides and storms has reduced the parking lot by half and made a serious cut through to the bay. A temporary gravel road has been laid and a beach nourishment program is in progress. During the winter, when the road washed away, school children from the Coast Guard station and the park on the north end, workers at the Sandy Hook Marine Laboratory, and park personnel had to be ferried back and forth. Courtesy of Gateway National Recreation Area, Sandy Hook Unit

191

Dune walks, owl prowls, bike hikes, moonlight strolls, canoe trips, and photography classes are but a few of the programs open to the public at Gateway National Recreation Area. Pictured here is a canoe cruise of a freshwater pond at Sandy Hook. National Park Service rangers Barbara Johnson (left) and Kathy Craig are explaining the environment of the pond. Courtesy of Gateway National Recreation Area, Sandy Hook Unit

Local communities run environmental programs for children. Here some boys are listening attentively. MAECOM (Monmouth Adult Education Commission); the Art Alliance; and the Monmouth County Friends of Clearwater, an environmental group started by folksinger Pete Seeger, use other empty army housing. The NOAA Fisheries Service occupies the old post hospital. The New Jersey Marine Sciences Consortium (representing New Jersey colleges), and Brookdale Community College operate environmental education programs from two deserted army buildings. A naval reserve unit holds weekend drills in yet another. Courtesy of Gateway National Recreation Area, Sandy Hook Unit

In 1926 the Carlton was built as a vaudeville theater in Red Bank. The 1,515-seat house was purchased from the Walter Reade Company in 1973, and today the non-profit Monmouth Arts Center uses it to present cultural programs to the shore area. Ballet, symphonies, national touring companies of Broadway plays, and children's programs are sponsored by the fifty-two-member organization. The price tag on needed renovations is $3 to $5 million. Courtesy of the *Register*

194

This recently restored depot is one of the oldest landmarks in Red Bank. It was built by the New York and Long Branch Railroad in 1878. The company received its charter in 1868 to construct a line from South Amboy to the Raritan and Delaware Bay Railroad near Eatontown, and on to Long Branch. Courtesy of Jane Grammer

The George Hance Patterson house is on Monmouth Street in Red Bank. Within the past few years it has been converted to commercial use and has housed a complex of gift stores; most recently it was converted to use as a restaurant. Courtesy of the *Register*

195

Some years the Monmouth County Hunt attracts as many as 10,000 spectators. The program consists of five steeplechase races sanctioned by the National Steeplechase and Hunt Association. Pictured above at the 1977 Hunt are Joan Bergman, *(left)*, on her horse Reign High, and Kristie Randle on Aragler. Courtesy of the *Register*

The Monmouth County Hunt Club was formed in 1885, a tradition begun by Peter F. Collier. The Monmouth County Hunt Meet, the annual race meeting held on the Middletown estate of Mrs. Amory Haskell, started in 1926. The Woodland Farm event is the most colorful fall spectacle, and was suspended only once, for four years during World War II. The station wagon tail gate picnics have become a tradition. In more recent years the race meeting of flat and steeplechase events has become a charitable event open to the public. Courtesy of the *Register*

196

The U.S.S. *Nitro* is one of three naval ammunition ships that operate out of the Naval Weapons Station Earle. The ships supply the Atlantic and Mediterranean fleets. Courtesy of the *Register*

The Charles of the Ritz Company has a manufacturing plant in Holmdel. The firm, a leading producer of fragrances and perfumes, employs 600 people; it is a subsidiary of the Squibb Corporation. Photo courtesy of the Charles of the Ritz Company

197

Dr. George Sheehan (*left*), of Ocean Grove is a nationally-known cardiologist, runner, and writer. His lectures and writings have opened new paths for sports medicine in our running conscious world. Among the first writers to articulate the rewards of running, he is the author of the medical advice column in *Runner's World Magazine*. Courtesy of the *Register*

Members of the Monmouth County Chapter of the Archaeological Society of New Jersey are pictured on a weekend dig at Turkey Swamp. John Cavallo, a contract archaeologist and club member, is seen in the foreground checking soil samples. Ralph Phillips, Ed Morton (with trowel in hand), and Mickey Cohen are considering the proper technique to unearth the hearth they have just discovered. Courtesy of Jane Grammer

The Shrewsbury Historical Society Museum, Education, and Research Center was dedicated on November 14, 1982. Located just behind the borough's municipal building, the center contains memorabilia and artifacts relating to the borough's history. It consists of a museum, library, and public meeting room. The center maintains an active educational program for the borough's elementary school children. Courtesy of the *Register*

The Monmouth County Historical Association was founded in 1898. From a modest beginning, with its only possessions a safe and a bookcase, housed in the Red Bank Library, the association has grown until it now possesses a beautiful home in Freehold. The museum and library of the Monmouth County Historical Association is a graceful Georgian Colonial reproduction, a two-story brick building with pitched slate roof, woodwork painted white, and an arched doorway. It was designed by J. Hallam Conover of Freehold and opened in 1931. There is a popular junior museum on the third floor. The library has a genealogical and historical research collection. Photo from the collection of R. Van Benthuysen

When Jersey Homsteads (now Roosevelt Borough) was established by the Farm Security Administration in the 1930s, it commissioned the late artist, Ben Shahn, to create a mural on the wall of the community center. The mural depicts the origins of the town. Over the years the mural became cracked and deteriorated. Through a community effort the mural was sent to Italy for restoration in 1971. It is now on the wall of the library of the Roosevelt Public School. Courtesy of the *Register*

The Garden State Arts Center,
established in 1967, is operated by the
New Jersey Highway Department. It is
situated in Holmdel on Telegraph Hill.
The Arts Center's season includes
special daytime shows for children,
ethnic community festivals, and benefit
affairs to help finance free program-
ming for children and senior citizens.
From June to September the center
features symphony, ballet, opera,
popular recording stars, and the golden
oldies, such as Sinatra, Liberace, and
Como. Courtesy of the New Jersey
Highway Authority

chapter 8

Paths To The Future: 1983-2000

Monmouth County is a relatively uncrowded, pleasant place to live, described by some as one of the best-kept secrets of the East Coast. Monmouth County will not always be so lucky if an effort is not made to harness the forces of growth in the county and channel development away from the fragile shoreline, the verdant farmland, and the few remaining stands of virgin woods. The county's land recently became fifty percent developed. Undeveloped, open-space land is being lost at a rate of approximately 4,000 acres per year. The population of Monmouth County in 1850 was 30,313 with a density of 64.3 people per square mile. By 1950, the population had risen to 225,327 with 477.8 people per square mile. The census for the year 1980 indicates that over 503,000 people now live here, creating a density of over 1,066 people per square mile. The growing population creates enormous problems. One of these is where to put the ever growing number of people without taking up all the open farmland and forest area for homes.

The recently published *Monmouth County Growth Management Guide* attempts to focus growth in areas already developed and preserve existing farmland and undeveloped space. The guide also steers development away from environmentally sensitive areas, like Burnt Fly Bog in Marlboro.

No doubt, the race for open space in Monmouth County will continue to intensify as various users compete for what land is left. While growth and change cannot be stopped, nor would this be entirely desirable, every effort should be made to maintain the quality of life by preserving our rich natural, historical, and cultural heritage.

The challenges that face the coastal zone of Monmouth County are many and varied. The importance of protecting, preserving, and restoring our coast must be given a high priority. A wide variety of beach experiences are available in Monmouth County, from the excitement of amusement piers to the splendid isolation of the dune environment at Sandy Hook. There is truly a place at the shore for everyone. This variety must be maintained.

When we think about how to protect the shore for future generations, we must start with its most vital resources—the ocean waters. In past years, fish kills, red tides, and sludge and garbage dumping have raised legitimate concern over our abuse of the ocean. We must set as a goal the elimination of dumping or discharge of all noxious materials into the ocean as quickly as possible.

The Monmouth-Ocean Development Council sees a bright future ahead for the shore area. In his New Year's message for 1983 the organization's president, Robert J. Oberst, Senior, remarked that Monmouth County is fortunate it has not suffered as some other geographic areas have during these times of economic dilemma. Oberst sees an opportunity for business to grow, and to provide employment in the decades ahead. ●

Bibliography

Beekman, George C. *Early Dutch Settlers of Monmouth County, New Jersey.* Freehold, N.J.: Moreau Brothers, 1901.

Brown, James S. *Allaire's Lost Empire.* Freehold, N.J.: Transcript Printing Co., 1958.

Cunningham, John T. *The New Jersey Shore.* New Brunswick, N.J.: Rutgers University Press, 1958.

Ellis, Franklin. *History of Monmouth County, New Jersey.* Philadelphia, Pa.: R. T. Peck, 1885.

Guthorn, Peter J. *The Sea Bright Skiff and Other Jersey Shore Boats.* New Brunswick, N.J.: Rutgers University Press, 1971.

History of Monmouth County, 1664-1920. N.Y.: Lewis Historical Publishing Co., 1922.

Hornor, William S. *This Old Monmouth of Ours; History, Tradition, Biography, Genealogy, Anecdotes.* Freehold, N.J.: Moreau Brothers Publishers, 1932.

Kobbé, Gustav. *The New Jersey Coast and Pines: An Illustrated Guide.* Short Hills, N.J.: Privately printed, 1889.

Leonard, Thomas. *From Indian Trail to Electric Rail.* Atlantic Highlands, N.J.: Atlantic Highlands Journal, 1932.

McMahon, Timothy J. *The Golden Age of the Monmouth County Shore, 1864-1914.* Fair Haven, N.J.: The author, 1964.

Moss, George H., Jr. *Nauvoo to the Hook; The Iconography of a Barrier Beach.* Locust, N.J.: Jervey Close Press, 1964.

Moss, George H., Jr. *Steamboat to the Shore; A Pictorial History of the Steamboat Era in Monmouth County.* Sea Bright, N.J.: Jervey Close Press, 1966.

Nelson, William. *The New Jersey Coast in Three Centuries with Genealogical and Historic-Biographic Appendix.* N.Y.: Lewis Historical Pub. Co., 1902.

New Jersey Writers' Program. *Entertaining a Nation, the Career of Long Branch.* Bayonne, N.J.: Jersey Printing Co., 1940.

New Jersey Writers' Program. *Matawan, 1686-1936.* Keyport, N.J.: Brown Publishing and Printing Co., 1936.

Phillips, Helen. *Red Bank on the Navesink.* Red Bank, N.J.: Caesarea Press, 1977.

Rose, T. F. *Historical and Biographical Atlas of the New Jersey Coast.* Philadelphia, Pa.: Woolman and Rose, 1878.

Salter, Edwin. *A History of Monmouth and Ocean Counties.* Bayonne, N.J.: E. Gardner and Son, 1890.

Salter, Edwin. *Old Times in Old Monmouth.* Freehold, N.J.: Printed at the office of the *Monmouth Democrat,* 1874.

Schenck, J. H. *Album of Long Branch, a Series of Photographic Views.* N.Y.: J. F. Trow, 1868.

Smith, Samuel Stelle. *The Battle of Monmouth.* Monmouth Beach, N.J.: Philip Freneau Press, 1964.

Smith, Samuel Stelle. *Sandy Hook and the Land of the Navesink.* Monmouth Beach, N.J.: Philip Freneau Press, 1963.

Stillwell, John. *Historical and Genealogical Miscellany; Data Relating to the Settlement and Settlers of New York and New Jersey.* N.Y.: Privately printed, 1903-1932.

Stryker, William. *The Battle of Monmouth.* Princeton, N.J.: Princeton University Press, 1927.

Symmes, Frank. *History of Old Tennent Church, with Biographical Sketches of its Pastors.* Freehold, N.J.: James S. Yard & Son, 1897.

Wilson, Harold. *The Jersey Shore: A Social and Economic History of the Counties of Atlantic, Cape May, Monmouth, and Ocean.* N.Y.: Lewis Historical Publishing Co., 1953.

Newspaper Files

The Asbury Park Press
The Register
The Long Branch Daily Record

Special Collections

The Durnell Collection of Illustrations, Monmouth College Library

Index

207